UITGAVEN VAN HET
NEDERLANDS HISTORISCH-ARCHAEOLOGISCH INSTITUUT TE ISTANBUL

Publications de l'Institut historique-archéologique néerlandais de Stamboul
sous la direction de
E. van DONZEL, Machteld J. MELLINK, C. NIJLAND et
J.J. ROODENBERG

LIX

MUṢṬAFĀ ʿĀLĪ'S *KÜNHÜ'L-AḪBĀR* AND ITS PREFACE ACCORDING TO THE LEIDEN MANUSCRIPT

MUṢṬAFĀ ʿĀLĪ'S *KÜNHÜ'L-AḪBĀR* AND ITS PREFACE ACCORDING TO THE LEIDEN MANUSCRIPT

by

JAN SCHMIDT

NEDERLANDS HISTORISCH-ARCHAEOLOGISCH INSTITUUT
TE ISTANBUL
1987

Witte Singel 24
Postbus 9515
2300 RA LEIDEN, NEDERLAND

ISBN 90 6258 059 9
Printed in Belgium

TABLE OF CONTENTS

FOREWORD

During the autumn of 1981 when I started to read the *Künhü'l-aḫbār*, 'The Essence of Histories', the magnum opus of the eminent Ottoman littérateur and historian Muṣṭafā ʿĀlī, I noticed that the printed edition of this work contains an incomplete version of the 'Preface' which Muṣṭafā ʿĀlī wrote to the Ottoman section of the *Künh*. Further research brought to light that only the Leiden manuscript of the *Künh*[1] seems to contain the missing text; it does not occur in any of the *Künh* manuscripts which I was able to see so far. What follows is a publication of ʿĀlī's 'Preface' in its entirety, making use of the Leiden manuscript. Some essential information about the writer, his work, and the characteristics of the text will be given. A synopsis of the contents and photographs of the Leiden version are added.

I should like to thank here, again, Professor B. Flemming of Leiden University who brought me into contact with ʿĀlī and his work, and who stimulated and advised me during my research. I would also like to express my gratitude to Professor C.H. Fleischer of Washington University, St. Louis, who was kind enough to send me a copy of his then unpublished dissertation and checked copies of two Istanbul manuscripts for me. He also took the trouble to read my transcription and pointed out mistakes or suggested alternative readings, thus contributing to a more satisfying interpretation of the text. Dr. J.T.P. de Bruijn, Dr. A.H. de Groot, and Mr. M. Hoos, all of Leiden University, looked at manuscripts in Upsala, Munich and Cairo for me and advised me; I thank them all. I am most grateful for the patient attention I received from the librarians in all the manuscript libraries where I worked, especially the Staatsbibliothek Preussischer Kulturbesitz, Berlin, the Österreichische Nationalbibliothek, Vienna, the Bibliothèque Nationale, Paris, and the Library of the Topkapı Sarayı, Istanbul. I am especially grateful for the expert guidance I received from Drs. J.J. Witkam, Curator of Oriental Manuscripts at the University Library of Leiden. Finally, my thanks go to the Nederlands Instituut voor het Nabije Oosten which has accepted this study for publication, and to its director, Dr. E. van Donzel, who provided invaluable advice in the final stage.

Jan Schmidt

[1] The manuscript (*L*) which represents an incomplete fourth *rükn* ('pillar') of this universal history, is kept in the Leiden University Library, *Cod 288 Warn* (M.J. de Goeje and P. de Jong, *Catalogus Codicum Orientalium Bibliothecae Academiae Lugduno Batavae* (*CCO*), III (Leiden 1865), 28, no. dcccl.

INTRODUCTION

1 The Writer

ʿĀlī was born in 1541 as the son of a well-to-do merchant and literary maecenas in Gallipoli (Gelibolu) and his more than average intelligence, literary talents and family relations made it possible for him to get the best possible education for a member of the 'common people', the *reʿāyā*[2]. In 1560 he successfully concluded his studies at the *medreses* of the highest, *ṣaḥn-i s̱emān* level (the 'Court of the Eight Colleges') in Istanbul, which entitled him to a career in the *ʿilmīye*, the learned hierarchy and Muslim administrative-jurisdictional institution of the Ottoman Empire. Although he always considered himself a member of the *ʿulemā*, he actually never became one, technically speaking. From the beginning he wanted to by-pass the long and burdensome career of an *ʿālim*. He tried his luck in Konya at the Court of Prince Selīm (who later succeeded Sultan Süleymān to the throne), and presented to him his first Persian *dīvān* (collection of poems). Although our writer was very proud of his literary accomplishments and, only 15 years old, had adopted the not very modest pen-name of ʿĀlī, 'the Exalted', he was not accepted as a court-poet, nor as an intimate companion, *muṣāḥib*, of the Prince.

In 1562/63 ʿĀlī petitioned directly for employment at the Court in Istanbul, but again to no avail. After this rebuff, ʿĀlī put himself under the protection of Muṣṭafā Paşa (d. 1580), a former instructor, *lālā*, of Prince Selīm. He became his private secretary and remained in that function until Muṣṭafā Paşa's death some 20 years later, most of the time dependant on the latter's patronage. In the same year (1562/3) Lālā Muṣṭafā Paşa was appointed *beglerbegi* (provincial governor) of Aleppo and ʿĀlī followed him there. Later he went with his patron to other posts, and stayed for short periods in Damascus, Egypt, and again Damascus. In 1568 Muṣṭafā Paşa got involved in a serious conflict with Ḳoca Sinān Paşa (d. 1595), the deputy military commander in Egypt, and with the latter's patron, Grand vizier Soḳollu Meḥmed Paşa (d. 1579). But he was soon rehabilitated under the influence of (now) Sultan Selīm (1566-1574), and promoted to *muṣāḥib*

[2] These and the following biographical data are mainly based on the dissertation of Cornell H. Fleischer, 'Gelibolulu Mustafa Âlî Efendi, 1541-1600. A Study in Ottoman Historical Conscience' (Princeton University 1982), which contains the most up-to-date and thorough-going description of ʿĀlī's life so far, see especially chapters I, II, and III.

and vizier in the *Dīvān* (Council of State). Possibly as a result of this conflict in which he was involved as a secretary, ʿĀlī could not profit from this move of his patron to the Capital, and a period of estrangement between him and Muṣṭafā Paşa followed, most of which he spent in Bosnia as a timariote *sipāhī* (cavalryman) and secretary to the *sancaḳbegi* (district-governor) Ferhād Paşa. After this 'exile', and after several appeals to the Court, in 1578 ʿĀlī was again appointed secretary under Lālā Muṣṭafā Paşa, who was now commander-in-chief in the war against the Persian Safavids. During the next years ʿĀlī followed him to the Caucasus-front and eastern Anatolia.

After Muṣṭafā Paşa's death in 1580, ʿĀlī was bereft of patronage, although he now and then received literary commissions and financial support from influential officials such as 'Ḫōca' Saʿduʾd-dīn (d. 1599), the well-known historian and personal instructor of several sultans, and Ġażanfer Aġa (d. 1603), the Agha of the Porte, both members of the 'anti-Soḳollu-faction' at Court. The rest of his life, mostly for very short periods, owing to the influence of his protectors at Court, he was able to spend as a middle-class official in the provincial administration. In 1581/82 ʿĀlī went again to Aleppo, now as *tīmār defterdārı* (administrator of the provincial fiefs), and in 1585/86 he was *defterdār* (director of the treasury) in Erzurum. In view of the income which he received: 140,000 *aḳçe* per annum, this was perhaps his highest post. In 1588/89 he was in Sivas, again as *defterdār*.

During the nineties ʿĀlī spent most of his time in the Capital, unemployed but working hard on his historiographical chef d'œuvre, the *Künhüʾl-aḫbār*, although he spent several very short periods in Anatolia as *yeñiçeri kātibi* (secretary to the corps of Janissaries) or *sancaḳbegi*. Finally, after three years without an official position, he was appointed *emīr* and *emīn* (district-governor and 'trustee') of Jedda, the harbour of Mecca. In July 1599 he left Istanbul for the last time and travelled to Egypt, not without the vain hope of becoming *beglerbegi* of this most important province. But after visiting the Holy Places in Mecca, ʿĀlī died during the first half of 1600 at his post on the Red Sea.

So much for some of the most important facts of ʿĀlī's professional life, a life that could not satisfy this ambitious and proud man. After a promising start and a precocious taste of court-life, his dependence on Lālā Muṣṭafā Paşa, which lasted almost twenty years, cut him off definitively from a career in the *ʿilmīye* and removed him practically from the centre of influence which was the Capital. His chances thus became very dim. His petitions for jobs and his dedication or bestowal of literary work — many of his ca. fifty works of poetry and prose[3] were written to woe potential patrons — did not result in a prestigious position

[3] See: Atsız (ed.), *Âlî bibliyografyası* (Istanbul 1968), 10.

in the centre of power (preferably that of *nişāncı*, the secretary of the Council of State who controlled the *tuġrā*, the sultan's official monogram which legalized official documents) in which he could turn his literary talents to account.

His early exile from Court and Capital, his difficult temperament which made him many enemies, and the uncertainty and spasmodic character of his later career embittered him, so that he was almost ready to retire from public life and give up his aspirations for good. His misfortunes he attributed mainly to a neglectful and disastrous disregard for tradition and literary talent on the side of the sultans who let themselves be influenced by, in his eyes, unworthy ministers such as Grand vizier Soḳollu Meḥmed Paşa. This, in his view, was an indication that the Empire was in a dangerous crisis following the ideal years of Sultan Süleymān (1520-1566)[4]. In this mood ʿĀlī started, during the nineties, to work on his History.

2 The *Künhü'l-aḫbār*

ʿĀlī began to work on his 'Essence of Histories' in the ominous millenial year 1000 AH (1591/92), two years after a violent insurrection of the Janissaries had shocked the Empire. This was followed by revolts in the provinces, while on top of that Istanbul was wrecked by devastating fires. ʿĀlī kept working on the 'Essence' until the summer of 1599, when he left the Capital for good[5]. The 'Preface' to the fourth part, the subject of the present publication, was originally written between the years 1597/98 and 1599. In the text itself ʿĀlī explained that in this 'pillar', as the four parts were called, he wanted to deal with Ottoman history up to the year 1006 AH (1597/98)[6]. In one of his lasts works, the *Mevāʾidüʾn-nefāʾis* ('The Table of Delicacies')[7], he wrote that he 'was busy annotating' the *Künh* up to the year 1008 AH (1599)[8]. The last major event, or rather series of events, which he describes in the *Künh*, was the Egri-campaign

[4] The bad influence of Grand vizier Soḳollu Meḥmed Paşa on Sultan Selīm II (1566-1574) and the crisis of the Empire are discussed essentially in the 'Preface', *L*, fol. 5a:9-5b:9.

[5] According to Fleischer, ʿĀlī shared up to a certain point 'the millenial mood' of Istanbul ('Âlî', 219), caused partially by the political (and physical) disturbances of the Capital and the Empire in general. The insurrection of the Janissaries, was the so-called *Beglerbegi*-incident of April 1589. It was called so because the anger of the Janissaries directed itself against the *beglerbegi* of Rumeli, Doġancı Meḥmed Paşa, a friend of ʿĀlī's, and *başdefterdār* Maḥmūd Efendi, who had been responsible for their being paid in debased silver. Both men lost their lives in the aftermath. This disruption, which was in fact a precedent, was seen by ʿĀlī as 'a landmark of imperial decline' (*ibidem*, 218).

[6] *L*, fol. 3a:16.

[7] The full title is: *Mevāʾidüʾn-nefāʾis fī ḳavāʿidiʾl-mecālis* ('The Table of Delicacies on the Etiquette of Salons'), facsimile edition by C. Baysun (Istanbul 1956).

[8] Lit.: '(...) till the beginning of the year 8 after 1000, the annotations (*taʿlīḳāt*) in relation with the writing of the *Künhüʾl-aḫbār* and the loads of work [it gave me] (...)', *Mevāʾid*, 7:7-9. Cf. Fleischer, Âlî, 327.

of the summer/autumn of 1596[9]. The 'Preface' mentions the surrender of the border-stronghold Egri (now called Eger in Hungarian), the main objective of the campaign[10]. At the end of this chapter, moreover, ʿĀlī writes that he had 'brought the writing of the four parts of the *Künh* (...) to its conclusion'[11]. This points to the fact that our 'Preface' belongs to the last 'annotations' (*taʿlīḳāt*[12] on which he worked, or is actually the very last addition which he wrote for the *Künh*[13].

The work was written in a time that proved indeed to crucial for the development of the Ottoman state. The almost continuous expansion 'from one to fourty *beglerbegiliks*[14], and the flourishing, after a period of about two and a half centuries, seemed to have come to a standstill and to be threatened by severe financial, social and cultural upheavals.

Although the real nature and even the dating of this crisis is still a matter of debate among historians, and although many contemporary Western observers felt that the Empire was still at the apex of its power[15], the fact remains that for a writer like ʿĀlī—he was not the only one[16]—a fundamental change for the worse[17] had set in during the fifties of the seventeenth century. A very important motive for writing the *Künh* was to draw a broad picture of the magnificent development of the Ottoman Empire and its idiosyncratic Muslim culture against a broad

[9] The conquest of the fortress, and the following battle in the plain of Mezőkeresztes (Haçova), are discussed in my 'The Egri-campain of 1596; Military History and the Problem of Sources', to be published shortly.

[10] *L*, fol. 8a:12.

[11] *Ibidem*, fol. 8b:17-18.

[12] Cf. note 8.

[13] See also note 79.

[14] *L*, fol. 4b:15-16.

[15] Cf. for example the Spanish writer Cervantes, who fought in the battle of Lepanto. He wrote: '(...) *la casa Otomana, que de un humilde y bajo pastor que le dio principio está en la cumbre que la vemos*', Don Quixote de la Mancha, II, 7.

[16] Selānikī (d. 1599), for example, like ʿĀlī a bureaucrat and historian, also criticized in his History the decay of the Ottoman state and the haphazardness of the contemporary career-system, especially of the Financial Establishment, of which he, like ʿĀlī, had become a victim. See: Fleischer, 'Âlî', 213-215.

[17] Fleischer points to a striking similarity between ʿĀlī's view on contemporary Ottoman developments (shared by other Ottomans) and the 14th century north-African historian Ibn Khaldūn's theory of state, as formulated in his famous *Muqaddima* (which was apparently not yet known by Ottoman scholars then). If Ibn Khaldūn's theory were to be applied to the Ottoman situation, the Empire would have been in its fourth state, that of incipient decline; both ʿĀlī and Ibn Khaldūn advocated measures of reform which would restore an earlier state of affairs that had proved to be successful; this meant for ʿĀlī 'a restoration of the standards and dynastic institutions of the early-to-middle sixteenth century'. A similarity in out-look of both scholars, Fleischer continues, is not so surprizing if we realize that both men were heirs of 'the islamicized synthesis of Greek and Iranian social thought'. See: C.H. Fleischer, 'Royal Authority, Dynastic Cyclism, and "Ibn Khaldûnism" in Sixteenth-Century Ottoman Letters', in: *Journal of Asian and African Studies XVIII*, 3-4 (1983), 215-217.

historical background, and to remind the sultan and the responsible *ʿulemā* and statesmen, ideally all men of letters, of their past and their duties[18].

The *Künh* was in the first place a desinterested work of learning for which the author was not commissioned and which in the end he did not dedicate to anyone[19]. It meant to deal with historical events and with 'true traditions'[20] and thus did not have the sustained moralizing tone and biting satire, often stylistically most virtuose, of many of his other works such as his *Nuṣḥatu's-selāṭīn* ('Council for Sultans') of 1581[21] and his *Mevāʾid*. The *Nuṣḥat*, in which he drew the attention of Sultan Murād III (1574-1595) to serious abuses in the Ottoman administration of his time, was conceived as a 'mirror for princes', but was free of many of the clichés of literary convention, often encountered in such moralistic works. It was based on his experiences as an official and also sometimes inspired by friendship of animosity towards persons with whom he had come into contact. The same is true for his equally famous *Mevāʾid*, ʿĀlī's last critical and detailed précis of contemporary Ottoman society.

But although the *Künh* as a whole was written in the more detached mood of the learned historian, it is the disappointed and angry official and *ʿālim*-manqué who speaks out when he touches the subject of the decay of contemporary Ottoman society, as he does in the fourth 'pillar', and especially in its 'Preface'. He then uses the same, often brilliant, literary devices to give vent to his moral indignation as regards the irresponsability of the sultan or the corruption at Court.

From the beginning of the seventies, when he wrote his *Nādirüʾl-maḥārib* ('Rarity of Battles') in which the conflict between the Princes Selīm and Bāyezīd, sons of Sultan Süleymān, was described, ʿĀlī composed some dozen prose-works on historical subjects. But nearly all of them dealt with contemporary Ottoman themes and none had the scope of his voluminous *Künhüʾl-aḫbār*.

The work was given the form of a universal history, a genre which had a long and prestigious tradition in the rich Muslim historiography and had been developed by famous authors such as aṭ-Ṭabarī (d. 923)[22] and Masʿūdī (d. 956).

18 Cf. Fleischer, 'Âlî', 324 and 459-462. On the decreasing role of the *ʿulemā* as historians and critics of contemporary society, see the 'Preface', *L*, fol. 5b:13-6a:3.
19 Cf. Fleischer, 'Âlî', 228. Late in 1595, ʿĀlī played with the idea of dedicating the *Künh* to Sultan Meḥmed III on the condition that he be appointed *beglerbegi* or even vizier (*ibidem*, 300). Nothing came of it, though.
20 'We have taken care not to relate traditions that are adorned with dim lies (...)', *Künhüʾl-aḫbār* (*KA*), 5 vols. (Istanbul 1861-1868), I, 10:11-13. Cf. Fleischer, 'Âlî', note 1. For further references to the printed edition, see p. 17.
21 Edited by A. Tietze, *Muṣṭafā ʿĀlī's Councel for Sultans of 1581*, 2 vols. (Vienna 1979 and 1982).
22 He is mentioned in the 'Preface', *L*, fol. 6a:12 and in the general preface, *KA*, I, 17:27.

Universal histories written in this tradition set out to describe the development of the world in a complete and mainly chronological way, from the creation of the universe, through the half-hidden and largely mythical pre-Muslim past, up to the events of the contemporary world, in which the dynasty to which the author felt loyal because of nationality, geography or patronage, occupied a final and important place[23]. The non-Muslim world, being irrelevant to God's historical purpose with man, fell in most cases outside the scope of the historian[24]. This is also the case with the *Künh* where non-Muslim history plays at most a very marginal role in the representation of events. From the 13th century on it also became fashionable, especially in Persian historiography, thus continuing the rich tradition of Arabic biographical literature, to devote more and more space to the biographies of mainly religious personalities of every period, often at the expense of the coherence of these works[25]. The History of Ibn Kaṯīr (d. 1373)[26] is a famous example of this development.

Ottoman men of letters were, of course, familiar with the classical tradition of Muslim historiography, and especially with the work of aṭ-Ṭabarī. The growing expansion and self-confidence of the Ottoman state and dynasty during the second half of the 15th century was accompanied by a strong development of its historiography. The traditional genres such as the straightforward and simple chronicle and historical epic, and also works written in Arabic or Persian, lost favour with the leading literary patrons and the Court. A new literary historiography, worthy of the prospering Empire and continuing both indigenous and Arabo-Persian traditions, came into being. It was written in a Turkish which had been enriched by rhetoric devices modelled upon those of the prestigious Arabic and especially Persian literatures. The first Ottoman author to write a world history was Şükrullāh (d. 1488)[27]. He did not avail himself of the new literary vehicle, the Ottoman Turkish, but wrote in Persian. This type of history-writing did not find many practitioners in the decades to follow. In the next century the *nişāncı* Ramażānzāde Meḥmed Paşa (d. 1571) wrote a world history in the now fully developed Ottoman Turkish, but it was short and not much more than a digest (*fihrist*)[28]. ʿĀlī had known him personally when studying in Istanbul; he admired his work and tried to continue it[29]. The *Künh* is virtually the first fully elaborated

23 See: F. Rosenthal, *A History of Muslim Historiography* (3rd impr., Leiden 1968), 135.

24 One of the most famous exceptions was the Persian historian Rašīdu'd-dīn (d. 1318). See: K. Jahn, *Die Frankengeschichte des Rašīd ad-Dīn* (Vienna 1977), 9-10. ʿĀlī mentions him in his general preface, *KA*, I, 19:14.

25 Rosenthal, *Historiography*, 148-150.

26 Mentioned by ʿĀlī, *KA*, I, 17:27.

27 V.L. Ménage, 'The Beginnings of Ottoman Historiography', in: B. Lewis and P.M. Holt, *Historians of the Middle East* (London etc 1962), 173.

28 Cf. *L*, fol. 6b:5-6.

29 Fleischer, 'Âlî', 50-51.

universal history written in the literary language. It covers the history from the creation up to the last Hungarian campaigns and is the first work to include extensive biographical sections on Ottoman grand viziers and other high officials, *'ulemā*, *şeyḫ*s and poets.

The work is devided in four parts, called 'pillars' (*rükn*). Its contents are roughly the following: the first pillar (corresponding with Vols. I, II and III in the printed edition) contains a general introduction and the history of the creation, that of the prophets, Muḥammad, his companions and the Twelve Imams. The second pillar (corresponding with Vol. IV-1) describes the history of the Omayyad and Abāssid Caliphs. The third pillar (printed in Vol. IV-2,3) deals with the history of the Tatar and Turkish dynasties, and the fourth (Vol. V) gives a more or less chronological history of the Ottomans until 'Ālī's own days. This fourth part includes an introduction and has biographical sections which are arranged according to the reigns of the sultans, with the exception of the periods of Murād III (1575-1595) and Meḥmed III (1595-1596, ruled until 1603).

The introductory part of the fourth pillar, of importance for our subject, is divided in five 'chapters', covering 14 folios in the Leiden manuscript[30]. The first chapter is an eulogy of God and the creation, and in particular of the Ottoman dynasty. The second chapter is the author's preface in which he gives his reasons for writing this part of the *Künh*. The third chapter is a short section on the origins of the Ottoman population in Anatolia and Rumeli. It also gives the outlines of the political, social and cultural history from the 11th to the 14th centuries. The fourth chapter deals with the different peoples living on the borders of the Empire who contributed to the formation of the Ottoman state through the *devşirme*, i.e. the levy of Christian children to be trained for posts in the Palace, in the administration or in the imperial military corps. The fifth chapter, finally, is an introduction to the 'science of physiognomy', and deals mainly with the status and titles of the Muslim rulers, especially with the three great Ottoman sultans Meḥmed the Conqueror (1444-1446 and 1451-1481), Selīm I (1512-1520) and Süleymān 'the Law-giver' (1520-1566)[31].

The basic 'facts' of 'Ālī's History are based on external sources, even when the author deals with contemporary developments, the more so since he himself virtually never occupied a position in the centre of power where (historical) decisions were made. Many of his written sources are listed in the introductory chapters to the first and fourth pillars. In the introduction to the first part 'Ālī mentions 130

[30] *L*, fol. 1b-14b.

[31] I: fol. 1b (*KA*, V, 2); II: fol. 3a (*KA*, V, 6); III: fol. 9a (*KA*, V, 8); IV: fol. 10a (*KA*), V, 9); and V: fol. 12b (*KA*, V, 14).

Arabic and Persian works, consisting of 'ca. 600 volumes', he 'had gone over'[32]. Of these, only three seem to have been written by Ottomans: the *Mir'atu'l-memālik* ('The Mirror of Countries'), written in 1553-'58 by Seyyidī 'Alī Çelebi, an unspecified work of the famous scholar and *şeyḫü'l-İslām* Ebū'ṣ-ṣu'ūd (d. 1574)[33] and the *Şaḳāyiḳu'n-nu'mānīye* ('The Red Peonies'), a biographical dictionary written in 1558 by Ṭaşköprizāde[34]. In the 'Preface' to the fourth pillar, 'Ālī gives a short outline of the Ottoman historiographical tradition[35] and mentions nine writers, from 'Āşıḳpaşazāde (d. after 1484) to Sa'du'd-dīn. In the second half of the chapter, he comes to speak of three contemporary and despised *şehnāmecis* (Loḳmān, Ta'līḳīzāde and Nuṭḳī)[36], court-poets who had the task of glorifying the deeds of the sultans in verse as the Persian poet Firdawsī (d. ca. 1020) had done about 600 years before in his epic *Šāhnāma*.

The names and works of most of these twelve writers are very well known and, from a few explicit quotations in the main part of the fourth pillar it is evident that 'Ālī used most of them as sources[37]. A possible exception might be the famous History of Kemāl Paşazāde (d. 1534) whose name occurs in the 'Preface', but to which there is apparently no reference in the main work. In his 'Preface' 'Ālī lists the *Cāmi'ü'l-meknūnāt* and it is known that he used it as a source[38], but its supposed author, a certain Mevlānā 'Īsā[39] has so far remained unknown, and I was unable to identify him further[40]. It has also been known, that 'Ālī used for the *Künh* the work of the *şehnāmeci* Loḳmān[41]. Finally, he may have made use of the writings of the other two, Ta'līḳīzāde and Nuṭḳī (if the latter's verse were ever committed to paper).

But 'Ālī's sources were certainly more numerous than the ones mentioned in the 'Preface'. He also used official documents that went through his hands, and

[32] *KA*, I, 17:21-22. The scrutiny was termed thus: '(...) *gözden geçürmek mertebeleri taḥaḳḳuḳ buldı*'. The works are enumerated in I, 17-19.

[33] *KA*, I, 18:12-13.

[34] *Ibidem*, 18:20.

[35] *L*, fol. 6a:3-6b:11.

[36] *Ibidem*, fol. 6b:20-8b:10.

[37] Cf. Fleischer, 'Âlî', 575, note 1.

[38] See: B. Flemming, 'Der *Cāmi' ül-meknūnāt*. Eine Quelle 'Ālīs aus der Zeit Sultan Süleymāns', in: H.R. Roemer and A. Noth (ed.), *Studien zur Geschichte und Kultur des Vorderen Orients* (Leiden 1981), 81.

[39] *L*, fol. 6a:7.

[40] The *Cāmi'* known to us must be dated between 1529 and, probably, 1535 (Flemming, 'Der *Cāmi'*, 84). Mevlānā 'Īsā does not occur in the *Künh* in any of the biographies of *'ulemā* of the reign of Sultan Süleymān as far as I could see (*Hs or quart 1090* (*B*), fol. 373b-388a; B. Flemming, *Türkische Handschriften I* (Wiesbaden 1968), 19, no. 26. The ms. is kept in the *Staatsbibliothek Preussischer Kulturbesitz* in Berlin).

[41] Cf. *KA*, V, 25:21. Loḳmān is wrongly spelt as Nu'mān, as happens also sometimes in the manuscripts.

availed himself of oral information[42]. However, further identification of ʿĀlī's sources, and the question how he used them (e.g. whether his statement in the general introduction, according to which he intended to use only 'true traditions' is more than a literary cliché), exceeds the scope of this study.

Not only form, contents and sources of the *Künh* (and the wider question of its historical reliability) merit our attention, but its language as well. As remarked above, it was a crucial element in the development of Ottoman historiography. A highly developed literary style, which meant the use of rhymed prose alternated with short poems, was of utmost importance for writers like ʿĀlī, as it indeed had been since the time of the later Persian prose-writers and historians. The historian Waṣṣāf (d. ca. 1330), with his famous 'History', contributed in particular to an increasing tendency among most later Persian prose-writers towards an 'exuberant embellishment and affectation' to the point even of 'monstruous bombast'[43]. Waṣṣāf was widely imitated by Ottoman historians who wrote in Turkish. From the late 15th century onwards, the Turkish language, borrowing copiously from the treasury of the Arabo-Persian vocabulary, developed its most prestigious and sophisticated variant. From the beginning of the sixties, when he wrote his first prose-work, the unfinished *Enīsü'l-ḳulūb* ('The Heart's Familiar')[44], ʿĀlī acquired an almost unequalled mastery over this type of language, and, above all, developed a personal prose-style that did not '[drown] in empty verbosity'. It varied widely 'from dry-factual narrative to the most involved *Kunstprosa* (*inṣā*)' and could sometimes almost explode in very 'direct and rude graphic images'[45], especially when ʿĀlī expressed his indignation about the decay of morality or the baseness of unbelievers.

In the general introduction to the first pillar, ʿĀlī stated explicitely that he intended to avoid bombast and to use a well-wrought style 'useful for both the élite and the common people'[46]. His pages were meant to be literature and to be recited in literary séances (*mecālis*), their first aim being the amusement of the audience[47].

[42] E.g. in 1578, during the war against the Safavids and their allies, ʿĀlī conversed with the ruler of Daghistān, and reported in the *Künh* what he heard about the Georgian tribes in the neighbourhood of Sulṭāncıḳ, the place where they met, especially their filthy eating and drinking habits and sexual mores (*L*, fol. 355b-356b, cf. Fleischer, 'Âlî', 238-239, note 22.). Examples of the first type are amply provided in the same part of the *Künh*, where ʿĀlī quotes from the war-correspondence he read and wrote himself as Lālā Muṣṭafā Paşa's secretary (*L*, fol. 338b-371a, *passim*).

[43] J. Rypka, *History of Iranian Literature* (translated from the Czech and edited by J. Jahn, Dordrecht 1968), 312 and 314.

[44] See for this work : H. Sohrweide, '*Enīs el-qulūb* : Ein verschollenes Werk des Historikers Muṣṭafā ʿĀlī', in : *VIII. Türk Tarih Kongresi* (Ankara 1980), 983-991.

[45] A. Tietze, 'Muṣṭafā ʿĀlī of Gallipoli's Prose Style', in : *Archivum Ottomanicum*, 5 (1973), 298 and 319.

[46] *KA*, I, 9 :27.

[47] *L*, fol. 5b :20-6a :3.

He considered the use of a sound literary style also of importance for historians in general. When he discusses Ottoman historiography in the 'Preface', he almost exclusively gives attention to this aspect. Kemāl Paşazāde was, in his opinion, the first Ottoman historian who 'wrote well, and expressed himself in a clear way'[48], and the same was true of Celālzāde (d. 1567), Ramażānzāde and, in particular, Sa'du'd-dīn[49]. These four historians, and 'Ālī himself, are nowadays generally considered as the great historiographers of the 16th century, and the *Künh*, especially its fourth pillar, is undoubtedly one of the most fascinating works of the age.

3 The 'Preface' to the Fourth Pillar

As said above, the author's preface, the subject of this study, is the second chapter of the introductory section of the fourth pillar of the *Künh*. It bears the traditional title *der sebeb-i te'līf-i kitāb* ('about the reason for writing the book') but, rather than giving 'Ālī's personal and scholarly motives for writing the volume, it offers a general introduction to the subject of the pillar[50].

The chapter begins with a short statement about the contents of the volume, and the author states that he intends to adhere to the traditional historiographical methods of his learned predecessors. The book is meant to be a history of the dynasty with a special regard to the activities of the *'ulemā*. Both points are elaborated in what follows. 'Ālī introduces the most important Muslim dynasties of his day, establishes their relations with the Porte, and enumerates the most important achievements of the subsequent Ottoman sultans, that is, their successful activities as expansionist warriors of the faith (*ġāzī*s). These paragraphs are followed by a short discourse on the decay (and threatening fall) of the Empire during the second half of the century, not unlike those to be found in 'Ālī's other works such as the *Nuṣḥat* and the *Mevā'id*. In his opinion, that deplorable situation was caused by the weakness of the last sultans who were unable to suppress corruption in the highest quarters or to check their greedy ministers. Three of these are mentioned by name, and it is clear that 'Ālī's disgust of at least one of these 'traitors' was inspired by personal experience. In 1569 'Ālī had asked one of them[51], the influential vizier and intimate of the sultan Şemsī Aḥmed Paşa (d. 1580), to find him a position at the Court in Istanbul, but Şemsī Paşa had done nothing and poked fun at him and his pretentious pen-name during one of the poetic séances in his house in Üsküdar which 'Ālī had attended[52].

48 *Ibidem*, fol. 6a:21-22.

49 See for his remarks on Sa'du'd-dīn: *L*, fol. 6b:7-11.

50 Cf. Fleischer's short survey in '"Ibn Khaldûnism"', 212-214.

51 *L*, fol. 5b:4-6. Se also *ibidem*, fol. 333b-335a ('fifth event' of the period Murād III).

52 This scene was described by 'Ālī himself in the *Nuṣḥat*, Tietze, *Counsel*, R 36ʳ, translated on 44-46.

ʿĀlī then comes to speak of the *ʿulemā*, who are neglecting their tasks, especially as advisers of the sultan. They do not warn him for the dangers which are caused by his retirement from active political life. What is more, ʿĀlī complains, erudition in general is declining. In former times, the memory of the glorious deeds of the sultans were kept alive by historiography and poetry being recited in literary séances. In a chronological way, he gives examples of nine Ottoman historians, some of whom are already mentioned. In the second half of the 'Preface', ʿĀlī in a derisive description, contrasts this tradition with the deplorable state of court-historiography of his own days, and criticizes the activities of the *şehnāmeci*s (or *şehnāmegūy*s as ʿĀlī usually calls them in a pseudo-Persian fashion).

It seems worthwile to go into some detail here, because these court-poets, in ʿĀlī's opinion, represent above all the way in which the central government, i.e. the sultan, are misled by greedy grand viziers and threaten to contravene the 'Old Law' (*ḳānūn-i ḳadīm*)[53] that stands for 'classical' Ottoman traditions as regards the order of society. Obscure persons, mainly from the East, 'blackguards' and 'jesters' in ʿĀlī's jaundiced view, succeeded in obtaining well-paid literary positions at the Court. This was partly the result of the long war against the Safavids, by which distances between the Capital and the East, i.e. the Caucasus and western Persia, had become closed in, and which had caused a large-scale immigration of *sunnī* intellectuals into the Ottoman Empire. Their appointment at the Court, like in the case of Loḳmān, had been stimulated by no less an authority than ʿĀlī's maecenas Ḫōca Saʿdu'd-dīn[54], himself of Persian origin. The time-honoured system of recruitment and selection through the *devşirme* and the career-tracks of the *ʿilmīye* were in this way circumvented, and highly qualified *ʿulemā*, such as ʿĀlī himself, were disregarded and had 'retired in bewilderment'[55].

The theme of the *şehnāmeci*s is also found in the section of the *Künh* that deals with the reign of Sultan Murād III[57]. There ʿĀlī speaks in general terms of the declining statecraft and patronage under the Sultans Selīm II and Murād III, who, in this respect, contrasted sharply with great predecessors such as Meḥmed the Conqueror and Süleymān the Law-giver[57]. Sometimes using the same vituperative deprecations as in the 'Preface', ʿĀlī attacks also here the intolerable role of the *şehnāmeci*s Loḳmān, Taʿlīḳīzāde and Nuṭḳī as court-poets and official chroniclers of the dynasty, although it is noteworthy that Taʿlīḳīzāde, indeed a member of the brilliant Fenārī family, is, eventually, in the 'Preface' (after he 'had swallowed his faults'), judged more favourably. They were not more than

[53] *L*, fol. 5a:15.
[54] See p. 13.
[55] *L*, fol. 6b:13.
[56] *B*, fol. 591a:16-593a:11; it falls outside the scope of *L*. Cf. Fleischer, ʿÂlî, 559-561.
[57] *B*, fol. 591a:17-592a:11.

'story-tellers', in contrast with the deceased Mevlānā ʿĀrif (d. 1562), their predecessor, who had been appointed by Sultan Süleymān and whom ʿĀlī had met during his studies in Istanbul[58]. He had known how to compose Persian poetry, while these incapable upstarts had acquired their positions only by sheer 'disregard for literary prose and poetry' at the Court and by way of a mere routine-measure[59].

The first to be attacked is Loḳmān (d. ca 1601)[60], an obscure person, who, as a foreigner, had acquired a bad name among [his fellow-]cadis'[61]. As the ultimate authority, it was of course the sultan who was to blame, but he 'who had always been besotted by wine' had suffered to be misled by the treacherous Soḳollu Meḥmed Paşa[62]. Loḳmān had remained in the imperial service for twenty years[63] and the sultan had squandered loads of tax-money on 'a regiment of painters and calligraphers'[64] who had settled at the Court to illustrate 'his (Loḳmān's) disorderly poetry'[65]. He had been able to acquire fiefs (*ḫāṣṣ*) at the value of 100,000 *aḳçe* per annum for himself and his friends (and this at a time when ʿĀlī's own financial position was often precarious), and every year he had rendered service to his protégés[66]. But he was not capable of writing poetry: 'According to his own opinion, he wrote until now 100,000 eloquent distichs, but some of them suffered from a [defective] metre, and most of them showed serious flaws in their contents and meaning'[67]. Several of his poems had even become popular, such as the verse recited when Sinān Paşa in 1573 had captured the Spanish fortress of La Golette (*El-Vād*) on the coast of north Africa. These verses showed serious defects:

[58] Fleischer, 'Âlî', 49-50, and H. Sohrweide, 'Dichter und Gelehrte im osmanischen Reich (1453-1600). Ein Beitrag zur Kulturgeschichte', in: *Der Islam*, 46 (1970), 290-292. Mevlānā ʿĀrif's work was not well received by all Persian and Ottoman critics.

[59] *B*, fol. 592a:11-17.

[60] He was appointed in 1569, F. Babinger, *Die Geschichtsschreiber der Osmanen und ihr Werke* (*GOW*) (Leipzig 1927), 164-165.

[61] *B*, fol. 592a:20-23. Cf. *L*, fol. 6b:21-23, where his appointment and supposed characteristics ('(...) *ḳużāt içinde ecnebīlik ile bed-nām olan bir şaḫṣ-i esmer* (...)') are described in approximately the same way. Cf. Babinger, *GOW*, 164-165. He came from Urmia in west Persia. See also: Sohrweide, 'Dichter und Gelehrte', 292.

[62] *B*, fol. 592a:23-24. Cf. *L*, fol. 7a:21-22, where the role of Soḳollu Meḥmed Paşa is confirmed. For the continuous consumption of wine by the sultan, see also: *L*, fol. 5a:17-18.

[63] *B*, fol. 592a:24-25. According to other sources he served 27 years as *şehnāmeci*, from 1569 till 1596 (Babinger, *GOW*, 164-165).

[64] *B*, fol. 592a:25-27. Cf. Sohrweide, 'Dichter und Gelehrte', 292. For his richly illustrated works, the *Şemāyilnāme* and the *Hünernāme*, see: N. Atasoy and F. Çağman, *Turkish Miniature Painting* (Istanbul 1974), 38-39 and 48.

[65] *B*, fol. 592a:26-27.

[66] *Ibidem*, fol. 592a:27-30.

[67] *Ibidem*, fol. 592a:30-32.

'Sinān Paşa āmed be-boḫlı deñiz
çe boḫlı deñiz belki āb leẕīẕ'
('Sinān Paşa came over the filthy sea,
the sea might be filthy, the water was delicious')[68]

Loḳmān rhymed *deñiz* with *leẕīẕ*: 'He had probably heard that there is no *ẕāl* in Persian. He put the *ẕāl* in the word *leẕīẕ* in an equal position as the *zā*, and rhymed [*leẕīẕ*] with *deñiz*'[69].

Thereupon he wrote his *Şemāyilnāme* ('The Description of Features')[70] in Turkish 'poetry and prose', as if that were the language in which he used to write'[71]. The book was accepted by the sultan, although the great Firdawsī would have turned in his grave if he had heard those lamentable imitations of his work, as ʿĀlī comments in the 'Preface'[72]. ʿĀlī then quotes a fragment from Loḳmān's work (the same verses are cited in the 'Preface')[73], and criticizes Saʿdu'd-dīn, whose History Loḳmān had used as the main source for his book[74]. At Loḳmān's request, the Ḫōca of the sultan had personally written a word of recommendation for it, so that his reputation had risen considerably but unjustly in the eyes of the learned[75].

After that, a secretary of the imperial *Dīvān*, Taʿlīḳīzāde (d. 1599)[76], a 'learned man, but, to speak the truth, suffering from madness'[77], was appointed member of the *müteferriḳa*-corps (the guards of honour of the sultan) and *şehnāmeci*[78], although Loḳmān was still working on his *Şehnāme*[79]. He had written only 'one distich in his life' and 'had become famous by two Turkish and one Persian

68 *Ibidem*, fol. 592b: 1-4, and Sohrweide, 'Dichter und Gelehrte', 292. For this historical event, see: Ş. Turan, 'Sinân Paşa', in: *İslâm Ansiklopedisi* (*İA*), X, 671.
69 *B*, fol. 592b:4-5.
70 The full title of the work is: *Ḳıyāfet* (or *Ḫāṣṣiyyet* as ʿĀlī has it) *el-insāniyye fī şemāyili'l-ʿOs̱māniyye* ('The Human Aspects of Ottoman Features'), written in 1588. It contains characterisations of the Ottoman sultans and short histories of their reigns (Babinger, *GOW*, 165-166), *B*, fol. 592b:6-7.
71 *Ibidem*, fol. 592b:7.
72 *L*, fol. 7a:23-7b:2.
73 *B*, fol. 592b:20-593a:11 and *L*, fol. 7b:22-8a:3. There occur some variations in the two texts.
74 Babinger, *GOW*, 166.
75 *B*, fol. 592b:24-30 and in the 'Preface', *L*, fol. 6b:23-7a:1. Saʿdu'd-dīn is called here 'a historian', but a comparison between the two fragments makes it clear that the same person is meant.
76 *B*, fol. 582b:34. He was in the service of Prince Murād before his accession to the throne, and Generally known as Kātib Meḥmed (Babinger, *GOW*, 167).
77 *B*, fol. 593a:1.
78 *Ibidem*, fol. 593a:3-4. C. Woodhead mentions that he was appointed 'around 1590'. This must be a mistake (*Taʿlīḳīzāde's Şehnāme-i hümāyūn. A History of the Ottoman Campaign into Hungary 1593-94* (Berlin 1983), 8).
79 *B*, fol. 592a:34. With this *Şehnāme* was meant perhaps the unfinished *Hünernāme*, written by the Sultan's commission, and not his *Şehnāme-i āl-i ʿOs̱mān* which had been finished by 1590 (Babinger, *GOW*, 166). Selānikī wrote that Loḳmān was dismissed in September 1596 because he had not written anything since the accession of Meḥmed III (Fleischer, 'Âlî', 253, note 71).

couplet'[80]. 'A *sersüḫan* (the coloured heading of a paragraph in a manuscript) of three lines, composed in literary prose, had sufficed to make him think that he had begun to compose poetry'[81].

But this was not all. 'While sensible intellectuals were suffering from the absurd favour showed to those two (i.e. Loḳmān and Ta'līḳīzāde) (...) there appeared yet another person (...), a certain Nuṭḳī[82], a Persian (or : dumb (*a'cem*)) Turcoman. He became a *şehnāmeci* of high rank (...) Although he was only a storyteller, he was deemed fit for the rank of *şehnāmegūy*. Although his source stood dry like those of his comrades, an imperial decree had taken him into service in the place of the mild Firdawsī of Ṭūs, and it had become evident that the difference between a *şehnāmegūy* and a story-teller had turned out to be non-existant in our time'[83].

They were not more than story-tellers, as 'Ālī had already pointed out in the 'Preface'. Not so he, who regarded his literary work as a serious occupation. In the beginning of the chapter he states that he had always done his utmost to seek 'divine inspiration' when 'travelling' over the pages that were like 'cities and large towns of black ink'[84]. For more than 52 years[85] he had roamed aimlessly about, 'while madmen sat in the *Dīvān* and he was left behind in the wilderness' as

[80] *B*, fol. 593a:1-2.

[81] *Ibidem*, fol. 593a:4-5. His poetic gifts were also sarcastically and at great length commented upon by 'Ālī in the 'Preface', fol. 7b:11-8b:7, although his Persian verse was relatively acceptable for 'Ālī, fol. 8b:4-7.

[82] Of Nuṭḳī nearly nothing is known from other sources. He is mentioned by Hammer in a list of 19 *şehnāmeci*s after Loḳmān and Ta'līḳīzāde (J. von Hammer, *Geschichte des osmanischen Reiches*, 10 vols. (Pest 1827-1835), I, xxxix). Perhaps he was appointed after the death of Ta'līḳīzāde on July 20, 1599, so that 'Ālī could have heard of his appointment just before his departure for Jedda in the same month. This would confirm the supposition that the 'Preface' (and the *şehnāmeci*s-section of the reign of Murād III) belongs to the last 'annotations' added to the *Künh*, if not the very last. In November 1601 Ḥasan Ḥükmī was appointed *şehnāmeci* (Babinger, *GOW*, 168). Nuṭḳī may have been dismissed or have died by that time. But perhaps Nuṭḳī was a 'non-official' (nichtbeamtete) *şehnāmeci* (cf. *GOW*, 164), employed at the Court at the same time as Loḳmān and/or Ta'līḳīzāde who were rewarded with fiefs for their activities (see : *L*, fol. 7a:16 and above, p. 12). To make matters even more complex, 'Ālī wrote in the 'Preface' that Nuṭḳī was appointed as second *şehnāmeci* after Loḳmān and before Ta'līḳīzāde, the third incumbent (*L*, fol. 6b:20-7a:7). It may be that 'Ālī was somewhat confused about the dates of appointment and the exact status of these court-poets, or his information must not be taken literally.

[83] *B*, fol. 593a:5-11. Cf. 'Ālī's designation here of Nuṭḳī as a 'Persian (or dumb) Turcoman (*Türkmen-i a'cem*), with that in the 'Preface': 'a (...) peasant who could be reckoned Persian in all his clumsiness' (*'acemligi ile 'acemlerden ma'dūd bir rūstā* (...)), where the author made a comparable paronymic pun with words of the same Arabic root *'ĞM*.

[84] *L*, fol. 3a:22.

[85] This points to the year 1593. It was in the spring of that year that 'Ālī retreated to his native town Gallipoli, to seek 'solace for his disappointment, and perhaps solitude and restoration', Fleischer, 'Âlî', 281.

he says at the end of the *Künh*[86]. However, after those years of slumber his eyes had been opened and God had made him able to write his History. He had brought this task to a good conclusion, not 'to please others'—and now, finally, we come to his personal 'motive to write the book'—but to provide the 'cold water of knowledge for the thirsty Muslims'[87]. ʿĀlī concludes the 'Preface' by expressing his hope that he and his work will find due recognition in this world and the next, that his History will be recited in literary séances in the future and that he be rewarded for it[88].

The 'Preface' as a whole, thus expresses in a concise way ʿĀlī's view on Ottoman history and the nasty turn it took, also for himself, during his lifetime. It is a balanced and condensed historical (and autobiographical) essay whose subject-matter and style, ranging indeed 'from dry-factual narrative to the most involved *Kunstprosa*' is quite characteristic of ʿĀlī. On the other hand, it does not offer us much unknown information on the author, his work or Ottoman history and historiography in general, except for a few details, such as the (supposed) name of the author of the *Cāmiʿü'l-meknūnāt* referred to above[89], and the persons and poetry of the three contemporary *şehnāmeci*s.

4 The Manuscripts of the *Künh* and the Leiden Fragment

The complete version of the 'Preface', the contents of which are sketched above, I have found so far in one manuscript only, namely Leiden *Cod 288 Warn*. All the other texts which I have scutinized so far, including the printed edition, offer a similar but much shorter version of this chapter, and lack a fragment of exactly five folios which does occur in the Leiden manuscript (fol 4a-8b).

Of the whole, or of parts of the fourth pillar of the *Künh*, 51 manuscripts are kept in libraries in Europe, Egypt and Turkey[90], dating from the early 17th to the 19th centuries, 35 of them containing the first chapters of this pillar. Until now I have

86 *Ahmed III 3083*, fol. 546a:10 (F.E. Karatay, *Topkapı Sarayı Müzesi Kütüphanesi yazmalar kataloğu* (KARATAY), 2 vols (Istanbul 1961), I, 240, no. 729, and Atsız, *Bibliyografya*, 112.

87 *L*, fol. 8b:16-17.

88 *Ibidem*, fol. 8b:18ff.

89 P. 8.

90 Manuscripts of the fourth pillar are listed in Babinger, *GOW*, 129, where references to the older literature can be found, and in Atsız, *Bibliyografya*, 24-28. See in addition: E. Blochet, *Catalogue des manuscrits Turcs*, 2 vols (Paris 1932), 37-38, 137 and 188 for the manuscripts in the *Bibliothèque Nationale* in Paris, and Flemming, *Handschriften*, 19-21, and K. Schwartz, 'Die Sammlung türkischer Handschriften in der Staatsbibliothek Preussischer Kulturbesitz (Berlin/West)', in: *Acta Orientalia Hungarica* (*AOH*) 37 (1983), 118, no. 10, for the Berlin codices kept in the *Staatsbibliothek*. Most Istanbul manuscripts are described, sometimes very summarily, in: KARATAY and *İstanbul kütüphaneleri tarih-coğrafya yazmaları katalogları* I, *Türkçe Tarih yazmaları* (*TTK*) (Istanbul 1943ff). Later research has enabled me to see nearly all of the 35 copies mentioned here (which include 9 copies not described in this literature). None of them contain in 'Leiden fragment' (August, 1986).

been able to verify 21 of them, among which the apparently oldest and most complete codex in existence (no. 1 of my list), which contains much material lacking in more 'standardized' versions[91]. These are:

1) *Istanbul, Süleymaniye Library, Fatih 4225*, 501 folios, copied in 1029 (1619/20).
2) *Berlin, Staatsbibliothek Preussischer Kulturbesitz, Hs or 8364*, 538 folios, copied in 1084 (1673).
3) *Berlin, Staatsbibliothek Preussischer Kulturbesitz, Hs or quart 1090*, 613 folios, copied in 1092 (1681) ('*B*').
4) *Leiden, University Library, Cod 288 Warn*, 385 folios, incomplete, copied between 1609 and 1674 ('*L*').
5) *Istanbul, Topkapı Sarayı Müzesi, Revan 1120*, 210 folios, first half, copied in 1084 (1673/74).
6) *Istanbul, Topkapı Sarayı Müzesi, Ahmed III 3080*, 773 folios, copied in 1088 (1677/78).
7) *Istanbul, Topkapı Sarayı Müzesi, Revan 1122*, 402 folios, first half, copied in 1143 (1730/31).
8) *Istanbul, Topkapı Sarayı Müzesi, Hazine 1359*, 275 folios, first half, copied in 1147 (1734/35).
9) *Cairo, Dāru'l-kutub, TTM* 27, 786 folios.
10) *Cairo, Dāru'l-kutub, TT 130*, 629 folios.
11) *Cairo, Dāru'l-kutub, TTM 29*, 480 folios.
12) *Cairo, Dāru'l-kutub, TT 28*, 350 folios, incomplete first half.
13) *Istanbul, Süleymaniye Library, Esad Efendi 2162*, 622 folios.
14) *Istanbul, Topkapı Sarayı Müzesi, Revan 1117*, 633 folios.
15) *Istanbul, Topkapı Sarayı Müzesi, Revan 1118*, 510 folios.
16) *Vienna, Österreichische Nationalbibliothek, H O 20a*, 487 folios.
17) *Berlin, Staatsbibliothek Preussischer Kulturbesitz, Ms or quart 1379*³, 335 folios, first half.
18) *Paris, Bibliothèque Nationale, S 1028*, 520 folios.
19) *Upsala, University Library, Cels 10a*, 469 folios, first half.
20) *Istanbul, Üniversite Kütüphanesi, TY 5959*, 589 folios, incomplete.
21) *Munich, Staatsbibliothek, 63 Quatr*, 268 folios, first half[92].

[91] Communication of Mr Fleischer, 31-8-1982.

[92] (1) Atsız, *Bibliyografya*, 24, no. 6; (2) Schwartz, 'Sammlung', 118, no. 10; (3) Flemming, *Handschriften*, 19, no. 26; (4) see: note 1; (5) Karatay, I, 238, no. 719; (8) *Ibidem*, 240, no. 728; (7) *Ibidem*, 238, no. 721; (8) *Ibidem*, 237, no. 716; (9) 'Ālī Ḥilmī ad-Daġistānī, *Fihristu 'l-kutubi't-Turkiyyati 'l-mawğūdāh fi 'l-kutubḫanati 'l-ḫidiviyya* (Cairo 1306), 218; (10) *Ibidem*; (11) *Ibidem*; (12) *Ibidem*, 217-218; (13) *TTK*, 22, no. 8 (7); (14) Karatay, I, 237-238, no. 717; (15) *Ibidem*, 236-237, no. 714; (16) G. Flügel, *Die arabischen, persischen und türkischen Handschriften der kaiserlich-königlichen Hofbibliothek zu Wien* II (Vienna 1865), 241, no. 1012; (17) Flemming, Handschriften, 20, no. 27; (18) Blochet, *Catalogue* II, 137; (19) C.J. Tornberg, *Codices Arabici, Persici et Turcici Bibliothecae Regiae Universitatis Upsaliensis* (Upsala 1849), 195, no. cclxxx; (20) no reference known; (21) J. Aumer, *Verzeichniss der orientalischen Handschriften der k. Hof- und Staatsbibliothek in München. Türkische Handschriften* (Munich 1875), 22, no. 73.

A part of the fourth pillar of the *Künh* was printed in the fifth volume of the uncritical edition of the *Taḳvīmḫāne-i ʿāmire*, published in 1861-1868 by Meḥmed Lebīb[93]. It was based on an unknown number of, presumably, Istanbul manuscripts. The volume breaks off halfway through the description of the second period of the reign of Sultan Mehmed the Conqueror, just before the description of the 'nine sieges' of Constantinople[94]. Some 500 to 600 folios were never edited in any form, except the last chapters of the fourth pillar, which deals with the first year of the reign of Sultan Meḥmed III. These are represented in only a small group of manuscripts[95], and were 'translated' into modern Turkish by Atsız in 1968[96].

The Leiden manuscript, which contains the complete version of the 'Preface', is described only summarily in the catalogue of De Goeje and De Jong of 1865[97]. Some more details will be given here. The codex consistes of 365 folios of 302 × 203 mm.; the text itself measures 233 × 127 mm. It has titles, names and quotations, mainly from the Arabic, as well as dots and lines in red ink. We find custodes all through the volume but they are lacking on some folios. The manuscript consists of 38 quires, most of them of five sheets (= 10 folios), as is normal for codices from the Middle East, although the 'Preface' is part of a quire of six sheets (= 12 folios, fol 2a-13b). Most quires show a slightly different hand, ranging from a very neat and regular to a more negligent *nesḫī* that goes in the direction of *nestaʿlīḳ*. The shape of the dots in red ink show also variations in the different quires. The number of lines amounts to 23 per page, although there is one page of 22 lines (fol. 101a). The paper is not always of the same quality, and has sporadically, but all through the manuscript, the same anchor-type watermark. Before the 21st quire, which begins with fol. 203, the paper is light-brown and varies between a glossy and a glossless quality. After fol. 203, it is both white and glossy. Between the 30th and 31st quire (fol 303b-304a), an important part of the book, consisting of about 25 quires, is missing. These probably would have contained the last part of the reign of Sultan Bāyezīd II, the complete reigns of Selīm I and Süleymān, and the major part of the period of Sultan Selīm II. The text breaks off

[93] The years of edition are generally indicated as 1277-1285 AH (1861-1868), but in the copy I saw in the Leiden University Library, the only year mentioned is 1277: *fī evāsıṭ-i ẕī ḳadʿa sene-yi 1277* (*KA*, I, 328). The name of Meḥmed Lebīb is mentioned in the same colophon, under whose 'humble supervision' (*niẓāret-i ʿācizāne ile*) this first volume was printed. M.S. Özge too mentions only the year 1861, *Eski harflerle basılmış Türkçe eserler kataloğu*, II (Istanbul 1973), 949.

[94] This 'chapter' occurs in *L*, fol. 147b. The last subject of the printed edition is the construction of the Aya Sophia in Constantinople, according to a 'second tradition', *KA*, V, 278 (in *L*: fol. 146a).

[95] Most 'complete' codices of the fourth *rükn* seem to stop after the first half of the description of Grand vizier İbrāhīm Paşa, e.g. in *B*. More complete versions are to be found in *Revan 1118* and *Ahmed III 3083* I saw in July 1983.

[96] Atsız, *Bibliyografya*, 52-112, based on *Esad Efendi 2162* and *Halet Efendi* 598, cf. 94, note 1.

[97] See note 1.

with the 38th quire, a normal one of five sheets, after, more or less, the fifth part of the '20th event' of the reign of Sultan Murād III[98]. The 19th century cover of the codex is of European origin and made of cardboard, but has a back and a large flap of leather.

The manuscript is part of the legacy of Levinus Warner (1619-1665), who lived from 1645 in Istanbul, mainly for his oriental studies. From 1657 onward he was also the official chargé d'affaires (*resident* in Dutch) of the Republic of the United Netherlands to the Porte. During his long stay in the Levant, Warner brought together a large collection of about one thousand, sometimes very rare, oriental manuscripts, that he partly bought, and partly commissioned to be copied in case purchase was impossible. The collection was bequeathed to the University of Leiden, and arrived in the Netherlands in 1674[99]. Some of the manuscripts, especially those that were copied in Istanbul (or in the Levant in general) may have been shipped to Holland as single, not yet bound, quires. This was obviously the case with a large part of the quires of chapters of the Bible, which had been translated into Turkish under Warner's supervision in Istanbul[100]. They were never bound and are still kept in that state in the University Libraries of Leiden and Amsterdam[101]. This may also have happened to the manuscript of the *Künh*, and would explain the missing of a large number of quires in the codex under discussion, namely of those that would fit in between the 30th and 31st, and after the 38th, quires. The actual volume was then bound much later. Although it is not possible to prove this, one might suppose that the missing quires were never copied in the first place, either because Warner did not have enough money, did not want to pay the price, or died before the job was done, or, if the whole work was in fact copied, that they were lost during the transport to Holland or somewhere between the 17th and 19th centuries.

If the book was copied on Warner's commission — in my view the most likely supposition — the Leiden manuscript must be dated between 1645 and 1665 (the period during which Warner was living in Istanbul) or even 1674 (when the last

[98] The 'event' breaks off after 1½ folio at the bottom of fol. 385a with *göndermişdür*, in *B*, fol. 530b:16. The '21st event' begins on fol. 534b. In *L* a large part of the reign of Murād III is lacking as well as the reign of Meḥmed III, corresponding with 83 folios in *B*.

[99] See: M.C. Juynboll, *Zeventiende-eeuwsche beoefenaars van het Arabisch in Nederland* (Utrecht 1931), 222-232 and A.H. de Groot, 'The Legacy of a Seventeenth Century Orientalist', in: *Prilozi za orijentalnu filozofiju* of the Oriental Institute in Sarajevo, 30 (1980), 159-165.

[100] See: M.E.H.N. Mout, 'Calvinoturcisme in de zeventiende eeuw, Comenius, Leidse oriëntalisten en de Turkse Bijbel', in: *Tijdschrift voor Geschiedenis*, 16 (1978), 577-582, and B. Flemming, 'Turkse discussies omtrent het Christendom', in: *Historische betrekkingen tussen Moslims en Christenen, Midden Oosten en Islampublicatie*, 9, 121.

[101] *Cod. 1107 Warn* in the Leiden University Library (*CCO*, V, 98-99) and *Oosterse Talen no. 49* kept in the University Library of Amsterdam (M.B. Mendes da Costa, ed., *Bibliotheek der Universiteit van Amsterdam. Catalogus der handschriften* II (Amsterdam 1902), 46).

pieces of his collection arrived in the Netherlands). If these dates are wrong after all, the earliest possible date of copying is 1609, for this is the first year in which paper with such an anchor-type watermark, found in some sheets of the codex, was produced in Venice[102]. In that case the Leiden manuscript could even be the oldest one of the *Künh*, older even than the Istanbul manuscript *Fatih 4225* mentioned above (no. 1), which was copied in the year 1619/20.

The Leiden fragment of five folios, mentioned above, is found between the words *meşhūr* (*meşhūrter* in *L*, fol. 4a:1) and *berḫōrdār* (fol. 9a:1). In the other 20 manuscripts which I was able to verify, as well as in the printed version (V, 7:16), these words are connected by *ve* into one sentence. This is a forced transition between two parts of the 'Preface' that bear no relation to each other. After a description of the qualities of the Moghul-emperor Jalālu'd-dīn Akbar, which is part of the enumeration of contemporary Muslim rulers, ʿĀlī, in a main clause that ends in the opative *taḥaḳḳuḳ ve ta'ayyün bula* ('may it be realized and become true')[103], puts himself abruptly forward expressing the hope that his reputation will endure.

In the Leiden manuscript, the first part of the sentence shortly after *meşhūr*, continues and ends with a predicate *idi*, in the same way as the sentences that precede and follow it. Here the enumeration of the Muslim rulers does not stop with Jalālu'd-dīn, but continues with the *şerīf* of the Hijāz[104] and the Tatar Khan of the Crimea[105]. At the other side of the 'gap', the above-mentioned wish of the author is part of a long sentence in the last section of the 'Preface', in which he begins to speak of his future fame. The optative *bula* is now, not surprisingly, and in a more natural way, dependant, albeit indirectly, on a principal verb *ümīd-vārum* (*ki*) ('I cherish the hope (that)')[106]. In this way, the Leiden manuscript, also from a linguistic and stylistic point of view, presents a much more satisfying text than the 'standardized' ones.

The question now remains why a large and indeed substantial part of the 'Preface' is lacking from a great deal of the manuscripts (if not all, besides *L*) and from the printed edition. One can imagine that the Leiden fragment, which is part to the *Künh* or a late 'annotation' to it, was rejected by ʿĀlī himself during the last revision of his work, at a time when there existed already more than one copy of the text, and that one or more copies containing the rejected version escaped his attention. This rejection could have been inspired by the fact that some of

[102] E. Haywood, *Watermarks, mainly of the 17th and 18th Centuries*, in: *Monumenta Chartae Papyraceae* I (Hilversum 1950), 63, no. 1, plate 1.
[103] *KA*, V, 7:19.
[104] *L*, fol. 4a:1-4.
[105] *Ibidem*, fol. 4a:5-7.
[106] *Ibidem*, fol. 8b:18.

the subjects he treated in this fragment, such as the deplorable activity at court of the *şehnāmeci*s, were already dealt with in other parts of the *Künh*. But this is only a guess.

It is in any case beyond doubt that the Leiden fragment was written by ʿĀlī; themes and style are undoubtedly his[107]. One might suppose that it originally belonged to another part of the *Künh* or even to another work by the same author, but this I consider doubtful. I have been able to verify that fol. 4-8, on which the fragment is written, were not added to the Leiden codex after the quires had been bound. They form a substantial part of the second quire of six sheets, all written in the same hand and on the same kind of paper. Moreover, the omission of the fragment from the text confronts us, as already remarked, with contextual, linguistic and stylistic difficulties. It is therefore quite unlikely that the omission is the result of a deliberate intervention of the writer himself. So we must conclude, at least for the time being, that the Leiden text represents the original (though perhaps not authorized) version of the 'Preface' to the fourth pillar of the *Künh*.

[107] As we have seen (p. 13), the same quotation from the *Şemāyilnāme* occurs in the 'Preface' and at the end of the fourth pillar, and one might compare the following two hemistichs:

vācib oldı ki ḥākim ola ḥakīm (*L*, fol. 5b:10)
maraż devāsız imiş ḥākim olmayınca ḥakīm (*Mevāʿid*, 33:7)

in which the same concept of the 'ruler' as 'doctor' is put forward by way of the rhetorical figure of paronymy (*iştiḳāḳ*). There are many other examples.

INTRODUCTION TO THE TRANSCRIPTION AND TRANSLATION

The transcription, and consequently, the translation of the 'Preface' are essentially based on the text of the Leiden manuscript (*L*), the numbers in the margin referring to the folios and lines of this codex. In some cases, however, indicated in the apparatus at the bottom of each page, I preferred, for reasons of style and meaning, to follow the version of the printed text (*D*), see the Introduction, p. 17. When the text was difficult, or impossible to read, or seemed corrupted, emendations and changes were also made in the original. These are annotated in the same way. There remained, however, some important difficulties, especially as to where the marginal additions of fol. 4a and 8a should be inserted into the text. The reading and translation of the satirical verse on fol. 8a:14-8b:4 was also not established satisfactorily. My solutions to these and other problematical points are tentative and remain open to correction, especially when more material will have come to light. All suggestions for a more acceptable interpretation are of course welcome.

As regards the transcription, I followed the conventions applied in the *İslam Ansiklopedisi* and used the 'classical' system of vocalisation, although there are indications some modern linguistic developments had already established themselves in 'common' Turkish as is clear from some slips of the pen of our copyist, e.g.: *plene bulunması* instead of *bulınması* (fol. 5a:8); *plene ʿaskeriniñ* for *ʿaskerinüñ* (fol. 4b:22); Acc. *naḳlını* for *naḳlın* (fol. 8b:9) etc.

For the Arabic and Persian quotations and fragments not incorporated in the Ottoman-Turkish linguistic framework, I applied systems of transcription more generally used by Arabists and Iranists. Fragments in red ink in *L* are in italics in the Transcription. In the Translation the orthography of names, titles etc. was sometimes adapted to a form more commonly used in English literature.

In the footsteps of the admirable ʿĀlī-editions of A. Tietze, I also tried to show, in the lay-out of each page, the rhyming structure of ʿĀlī's prose, which facilitates the structural analysis and the understanding of the often very long and complicated sentences.

In the Translation I tried to follow the original as closely as possible, and did not go into any trouble to convey the poetic qualities of ʿĀlī's prose and poetry. Without severely impairing the quite straightforward and lucid style of the author, such an attempt would have remained quite unsatisfactory.

Finally the scansion of the poems that occur in the text may follow here. The numbers refer to my 'Synopsis of the Contents'.

(3)	⏑ – ⏑ – | ⏑ ⏑ – – | ⏑ – ⏑ – $\overset{\cup\cup}{-}$ –	(*müctes̱s̱*)
(15)	– ⏑ – – | ⏑ – ⏑ – | $\overset{\cup\cup}{-}$ –	(*ḫafīf*)
(27)	Idem	
(29)	– – ⏑ – | – – ⏑ – | – ⏑ – $\overset{\cup\cup}{-}$	(*recez?*)
(31)	– ⏑ – – | ⏑ ⏑ – – | $\overset{\cup}{-}\overset{\cup}{-}$ –	(*hezec*)
(33)	– ⏑ – – | ⏑ ⏑ – – | $\overset{\cup\cup}{-}$ –	(*remel*)
(35)	⏑ – ⏑ – | ⏑ ⏑ – – | ⏑ – ⏑ – | $\overset{\cup\cup}{-}$ –	(*müctess*)
(38)	⏑ – – | ⏑ – – | ⏑ – – | ⏑ –	(*mütek̤ārib*)
(40)	Idem	
	⏑ – – – | ⏑ – – – | ⏑ – –	(*hezec*)
(41)	⏑ – – | ⏑ – – | ⏑ – – | ⏑ –	(*mütek̤ārib*)
(42)	Idem	
(43)	Idem, in both poems	
(47)	– ⏑ – – | ⏑ – ⏑ – | – –	(*ḫafīf*)[1]
(50)	– ⏑ – – | ⏑ – – | $\overset{\cup\cup}{-}$ –	(*ḫafīf*)

[1] The first hemistich of the second couplet does not fit in.

TRANSCRIPTION OF THE PREFACE

(3a:15) *der sebeb-i te᾿līf-i kitāb*
ve bā῾iṡ-i taṣnīf-i müstetāb
ki
āl-i ῾Osmān olan
mülūk-i cihān-bānuñ ḥaseb ü neseb-i memdūḥu᾿ṣ-ṣıfātları
ve sene-i seb῾ami῾e-i hicrī evvelinden
sene-i sitt ve elf tāriḫine dek
ẓuhūra gelen sülāle-i cihād iṡbātları
ve kendülere mu῾āṣır olan mülūk-i eṭrāfuñ min cihetü᾿n-nesl ẓuhūr u ṡebātları
ve kürsī-i memleketlerindeki temekkün-i ḥükūmet simātları
ḫuṣūṣan ḥüsn-i terbiyetlerine muḳārin olan ba῾ż-i ῾ulemā eṣnāfınuñ mücmelen āṡār u te᾿līfāt-ları
beyānında
ve ol ḥavādiṡüñ edā-vi mūcizle i῾lānındadur
(20) sebbāḥ-i deryā-yi zaḫḫār-i midād
ki
ġavvāṣ-i ῾ummān-i ilhām u imdād olub
ṣadef-i miḫbere vü devātdan
vāridāt cevāhirin çıḳarub
bāzār-i revāc u i῾tibār
ve reh-güẕār-i naḳḳādān u ṣayrefiyyān-i ẕevī᾿l-enẓārda
῾arż-i naḳd edegelmişdür
ve seyyāḥ-i müdün ü emṣār-i sevād
ki
be-vādī-i kerd-i rüşd ü sedād
ve nevāḥī-i nūr u fikret ü fu᾿ād olub
mā verā᾿-i baḥr-i muḥīṭ ü żulemāt
(3b:1) ve ḳa῾r-i jerf-i basīṭ ü mürekkebātdan
ḳaṭarāt-i āb-i ḥayāt nevādirin ḥāṣıl ḳılub
hünerverān-i dār u diyār
ve ḫıred-perverān-i a῾ṣār u rūzgāra
῾arż-i ῾aḳd-i gevher-i ῾ıḳd edegelmişdür

18 memleketlerindeki ... simātlari *L*: memleketlerinde ḥükūmet ü simātlari *D* | terbiyetlerine *L*: tedbīrlerinde *D* | 19 ve *L*: vac *D* | 20 sebbāḥ *L*: seyyāḥ *D* | miḫbere *L*: mühayyire-i *D* 2 rūzgār *L*: rūzgār der *D*

li-münşī'ihī

siyeh ʿamār ile döndi āl-i ʿAbbāsa
    beyāża çıḳdı öñinde sevād her ḫāme
dilinde ṭayy-i lisān ṭaylasānı başında ʿiyān
    müdām elinde ʿaṣā feylesūf-i ʿallāme
meger göñülden ve dilinden ʿibaret olmışdur
    iki dilinden ėrer naẓm u nes̱ri encāma
pür olsa anber-i ḫām ile ḳav mecmeresi
    muʿaṭṭar olmaġa başlar dimāġ-i hengāme
meger ki ḫāmedür ol naḫl-i mīvedār-ṣıfat
    yanında merdüm-i nā-puḫtenüñ döner ḫāme

bāʿis̱-i tasṭīr olan feḥvā-yi ġarrāyı
bu yüzden imlā ḳıldı
ve sebeb-i ḥādis̱-i taḥrīr-i ṣunūf ʿadd olunan mażmūn-i dil-küşāyı
bu ṭarīḳla inşā eyledi
ki
tārīḫ-i taṣnīf ü te'līf
ki
ḥisāb-i müstetāb-i hicrīde
tamām *elfe* elīf
ve ḥavādis̱-i ʿulvī vü süflī maʿlūm
her vażīʿ ü şerīf olmışidi
(margin) ve müʾerriḫān-i mülk-i Rūm
ve nükte-perdāzān-i z̲evī'l-mefhūm
ki
ferden ferden *wa mā minnā illā lahu maqāmun maʿlūm* mūcebince
merātib-i ʿaliyye-i ʿilmiyyede
ṣāḥib-i ḳavānīn ü rüsūm olduḳları
ḫuṣūṣan s̱emretü'l-ʿulūmi'l-ʿamelü bi'l-maʿlūm ravżasınuñ eşcār-i müs̱mire-i müstemirresinden
z̲ihn-i pāklarını
nevbāve-çīn bulduḳları
aḫbār u ās̱ārla
sükkān-i memālik-i ġabrā

siyeh *L*: siyāh D | ʿamār *L*: ʿammāme *D* | 3 beyāza … hāme *L*: müdām beyāża çıḳdı sevād her ḫāme D | ṭaylasānı *L*: ṭaylasān *D* | müdām *L*: hemān *D* | 4 dilinden *L*: dilden *D* | nes̱ri: nes̱r *D* neşri *L* | 5 döner *L*: ṭutar *D* | 6 olunan *L*: ohnan *D* | 8 şerīf olmışidi *D*: şerīf ki olmışdı *L* | 8 margin *mā D*: vac *L*

ve sākinān-i mele᾿-i aʿlānuñ gūşları ḍolmışidi
lā siyyemā
(8) selāṭīn-i mesālik-i rūy-i zemīn
ve ḫavāḳīn-i memālik-i maʿmūre-arażīn
yaʿnī
(10) aṣḥāb-i ḫutbe vü sikke nāmındaki şehriyārān-i mesānid-nişīn
ez merzübūm-i Rūm-i pür-temkīn
tā serḥadd-i Hind ü Ḫaṭā vu Çīn
kimler idügi
ve ne maḳūle kīş ü dīn
ü tertīb ü āyīn
ü aḥkām u ḳavānīnle
meşhūr idükleri
şüyūʿ-i küllī bulmışidi
bu minvāl-i ṣiḥḥat-me᾿āl üzere
ki
dāru᾿l-mülk-i *Ḳosṭanṭiniyye*de taḫt-nişīn olan zübde-i ʿOṣmānīyān
ṣāḥib-i tāc u negīn
sulṭān Murād Ḫān bin sulṭān Selīm Ḫān-i
mağfiret-ḳarīn idi
ki
üç yüz yıldan berü
ḫüdāyigān-i cihān olan tāc-dārān-i ḳavī-i temkīn
silsile-i celilesinden on ikinci şehriyār-i kām-baḫt u kām-bīn
idi
(15) niteki sākin-i pāytaḫt-i *Ḳazvīn*
ve memālik-i ʿAcem sevādındaki şehriyār-i ṣadr-nişīn
şāh ʿAbbās ibn-i Ḫudābanda bin şāh Ṭahmāsb-i riḥlet-güzīn olub
yüz yıla ḳarīb ḥükūmet ėdenlerüñ
yedincisi bir Ḫusrev-i mesned-nişīn
idi
baʿdemā Buḫārā mülkinüñ fermān-rānı
ve *Semerḳand* kürsīsinüñ ṣadr-nişīn-i ṣāḥib-i nişānı
mülūk-i Özbekiyyeden
ʿAbdu᾿llāh Ḫān bin İskender Ḫān olub
yüz elli yıldan berü
icrā᾿-i aḥkām ėden ṣāḥib-ẓuhūr

8 margin ḍolmışidi *D*: vac *L* | 9-10 ve … mesānid-nişīn *L*: vac *D* | maʿmūre-arāżīn: ma ʿmūre-i arżayn *L* | 11 -le *L*: ile *D* | bulmışidi *D*: bulmışdı *L* | 13 ki *L*: vac *D* | 14 ikinci *D*: iki *L* | 15 pāytaḫt *L*: taḫt-i pāy *D* 16 ibn-i *L*: bin *D* | 17 baʿdemā *D*: baʿdehü mā *L* | 19 icrā᾿-i *D*: enczā᾿-i *L* | ėden *L*: ėderdi *D* |

(20) *Ebū'l-ḫayr Oġlan* demekle meşhūr
melik-i büzürgvār evlādinüñ
on ikincisi bir kār-fermāy-i müteşerri' ü ḳavī-i dīn
idi
ammā mülūk-i Hindüñ cümleden eşheri
ḫuṣūṣan Timur-i ṣāḥib-ẓuhūr neslinüñ beşinci şehriyār-i nāmveri
sulṭān Celālu'd-dīn bin sulṭān Hümāyūn olub
nesli iki yüz yıldan berü
rāyān-i Hind miyānında
ekber ü muẓaffer ü kemāl-i
cūd u saḫā-ile
ve beẕl-i baḫşiş ü 'aṭā birle
(4a:1) cümleden meşhūrter bir pādişāh-i celālet-destgāh-i berterīn
idi
bunlardan mā'ādā şerīf-ile emīn
ve ḥākim-i Mekke-i mükerreme-i güzīn
ṣaḥīḥü'n-neseb-i nāmdār
u ṣarīḥu'l-ḥaseb-i bülend iştihār
re's-i elfe dek dört yüz yıldan berü
salṭanati ber-ḳarār
ve ḫutbe vü sikkesi şöhre-i dār u diyār
şerīf *Ḥasan bin Ebū Nümey* olub
āl-i Ṭāhā vu Yāsīn
ve sülāle-i sāmiyye-i ḫayru'l-mürselīnden
yigirmi yedinci rütbedeki mesned-nişīn-i
mekārim- nigīn
idi
(5) la siyyemā pāytaḫt-i Ḳırım Ḫānı
baḳiyye-i āl-i *Cengizüñ* devletmend ẕī şānı
Ġāzī Giray Ḥassān bin Devlet-Giray Ḫān olub
ol nesl-i büzürgvārdan olan
ḥukkām-i Tatār
ve mülūk-i 'ālī-tebār gāhında
(margin) olanlardan
tārīḫ-i hicrīnüñ sekiz yüz elli dördinci yıldan
mütemellik olan
maḥmūd Ḥāccī Ḫāna varınca

22 şehriyār-i nāmveri *L*: şehriyārı *D* | berü *L*: ziyāde *D* 23 ve *L*: vac *D* | beẕl-i ... 'aṭā *D*: beẕl ü baḫşiş-i 'aṭā *L* | 1 meşhūrter *L*: meşhūr *D* | bir ... ẕātınla (8b: 23) *L*: vac *D* | margin Ḥāccī: ḫōca *L*

yigirmi altı ḫānān ʿamūdında dāḫil olan
Mengli Ḫāna
nihāyet bulınca
onıncı sehriyār-i ġazā-kirdār-i memālik-sitān idügi
yaʿnī ki
ṭanṭana-i ʿanʿane ile
(7) yigirmi altıncı ḫān-i kār-fermay-i ḳavī-i temkīn
idi
egerçeki bu ẕikr olınan ḫān-i ẕī şān
ve şerīf-i Mekke-i mükerreme nāmındaki ṣāḥib-i ḳadr u ʿunvān
sikke vü ḫutbe ile meşhūr-i ālemiyān
iki şehriyār-i nāmdār-i memālik-sitāndur
lākin selāṭīn-i āl-i ʿOṣmāna ʿarż-i ʿubūdiyyet ėdüb
ve ḳırāʾat-i ḫutbe-i rafīʿatü ʾr-rütbede
(10) kendüler mülūk-i ʿOs̱mānīden ṣoñra
ẕikr olınub
sancaḳların çekmege muʿtād
ve evāmir-i ʿāliyyelerine muṭīʿ ü münḳād
ve serīr-nişīn olmada
daḫı anlaruñ iẕn-i şerīflerine gerdān-nihād
iki tācdār-i lāzimüʾl-iʿtibār-i ḳavī-i mürād idükleri
ʿiyāndur
maʿa ẕālik şāh-i mülk-i ʿAcem
ve ḫāḳān-i Türk-i maʿālī- himem
gāh u bī-gāh duʿā-nāmeler göndermek
ve ʿarż-i ḫulūṣ u maḥabbetle mütābaʿat göstermek
her āyīne ẓāhir ü nümāyāndur
ancaḳ bu şerefden ḫırmān
Celāluʾd-dīn Ekber ḫuṣūṣında vāḳiʿ
zīrā ki āmed-şüd-i elçiyāna buʿd-i mesāfe māniʿ
add olınduġı
(15) ʿarż-i iʿtiẕār yine bürhāndur
pes tārīḫ-i merḳūmda selāṭīn-i ehl-i islām
ve ancaḳ bu ẕikr olınan ḫavāḳīn-i ʿiẓām lāzimüʾl-iʿẓām
ḫarāc-güzārān-i
ʿatabe-i ʿulyāları nāmındaki rüʾesā-yi küffār-i nā-fercām
yaʿnī ki İspanyol ve Françḳo ve Rim Pab u Lüterān
ʿAndi-i Gürcistān u Çerkes ü Dādyān
ve Erdel ü Eflaḳ u Rūs u Boġdān
ve Leh ü Çeh ve Çar u Engürus u Alemān

ʿamūdında: ʿamūdesinde *L*

şāh-i hümā iṭā'atinde cünbān u ġalṭān
ve i'lān-i 'ubūdiyyet vādīlerinde dāmen der miyān
idükleri
ma'lūm-i enām-i eyyāmdur

li-münşī'ihī

şehriyārān-i āl-i 'Os̱mānı
kirdigār ėtdi ḫādimü'l-ḥaremeyn
memleket şeref ü 'izzin isteseler
żabt ėderlerdi hemçu ẕū'l-ḳarneyn
kılsalar serkeşānı da'vet eğer
kim 'alā'r-re's urur kimi ve'l-'ayn
āb-i tīġ ortalıḳda cārīdür
olamaz anlaruñla kes mā-beyn
pāyimāl olmazsa yollarına
merd-i ẕī şāna yüz ṭutar nėçe şeyn
terk-i cān farż-i 'ayn olur mes̱elen
ṣanasın vācibü'l-edā bir deyn
(4b:1) ḫāk-i dergāhına yüz sürendür
ecmelü'l-cihete ekmelü'l-'ayneyn

el-ḳıṣṣa
memdūḥ-i rū-şināsān olan
mülūk-i āl-i 'Os̱mān
ki
'Os̱mān Dāver Ḫān
ve Murād Ḫān
ve Yıldırım Bāyezīd Ḫān
ve sulṭān Meḥemmed Ḫān
ve sulṭān Murād Ḫān
ve Ebū'l-fetḥ sulṭān Meḥemmed Ḫān
ḫuṣūṣan Ebū'l-kerāme sulṭān Bāyezīd Ḫān
ve Mıṣr-i Ḳāhire fātiḥi sulṭān Selīm Ḫān
ve veled-i sa'īd-i reşīdi sulṭān Süleymān Ḫān
ve sarāylaruñ ferzend-i 'izzetmendi Selīm Ḫān
ve ḫalef-i ṣāḥib-şerefi sulṭān Murād Ḫān
ki

1 sürendür: sürendür olan *L*

zamān-i salṭanatlarında tamāmī mülk-i Rūm
ve ābrūy-i merzūbūm olan
büldān-i fesīḥatu'l-ercā
ve ekser sevād-i diyār-i 'Arab
ve kāffe-i Mıṣr u Şām u Ḥaleb gibi vilāyāt-i eyālet-nümā
'alā'l-ḫuṣūṣ ḥaremeyn-i şerīfeyn
ve nevāḥī-i Yesrib ü Baṭḥā
ve aḳālīm-i Yemen ü 'Aden ü Ḥabeş ü Baṣra u Laḥsā
lā siyyemā Cezīre-i Ekrād u Mōṣul u Diyārbekir ü 'Irāḳ-i 'Arab
u Azerbeycān
ve mülk-i Şirvān
ve kāffe-i müdün ü emṣār-i Gürcistān
u Dadyān
u Ḍaġıstān
ma'a zālik Cezāyir-i ġarb u Ḫalḳu'l-vād u Tūnis ü Ṭarablūs-ġarb
u Cezāyir-i Ḳıbrış u Rodes eyāletleri
mine'l-ibtidā ilā'l-intihā
ve āmme-i mużāfāt u mülḥakātınuñ ḥükūmetleri
mine'l-aḳāṣī ilā'z-zürveti'l-ḳuṣvā
ve silsile-i celīlenüñ selāsil-i fetḥ ü tesḫīre çekilmiş
mażbūṭları
ve ḳuvvet-i ḳāhire ile ümerā vu tuvānıñ
silk-i żabṭ u taṣarruflarına münselik maḥkūm u merbūṭları
olmışdur
ma'a zālik tārīḫ-i elfde vāḳı'
on ikinci baṭınla ṣābi'
sulṭān Murād-i sāliṣ 'unvānı ile baḫt-i nūr-efrūz-i 'ālem-gīrī lāmı'
şehriyār-i cihān-penāh
bir pādisāh-i 'ālīcāh u muẓaffer-i sipāhdur
ki
ḳalemrev-i ḥükūmeti
ḳırḳ miḳdārı beglerbegiligi şāmil
ve üç yüz ziyāde sancaḳbeglerini müştemildür
ḥālā ki cedd-i büzürgvārı *'Osmān Ḫān*
mücerred Anaḍolı beglerbegiligi 'add olınan
vilāyete fermān-rān idi
dördinci ḳarında vāḳı'
Timur ṣāḥib-ẓuhūr fitnesi ile ṣābı'
Yıldurum Bāyezīd Ḫān 'aṣrına gelince

17 ṣāḥib: ḥāṣib *L* 23

ḳalem-rev-i ḥükūmetleri ancaḳ Ḳaraman u Rūm
ve Rūmėli begleri begiligi ile mersūm olan
memleketleri ile ẓāhir ü ʿiyān
idi
ammā yedinci nesl-i şerīfleri
ki
Ebūʾl-fetḥ-i kişver-sitān Ḳosṭanṭiniyye fātiḥi
sulṭān *Meḥemmed Ḫāndur*
Rūmėli vilāyetini Bosna sınurına dek
Anaḍolı memleketini tevsīʿ-i tesḫīr ėdüb
diyār-i ʿArab serḥaddına dek
açdı
ve nėce ḥākim ü tācdāruñ ser ü efserini ḫāka yeksān ėdüb
diyār-i ʿAcem şehriyārı Uzun Ḥasan gibi
ḳavī vü ġavīnüñ ḥaḳḳından gelüb
ḫuṣūṣan ümerāʾ-i ʿaskeriniñ ḳanını ḫāk-i siyāha
saçdı
niteki ḳarn-i tāsiʿdeki *sulṭān Selīm Ḫān*
zamān-i devletinde
(5a:1) Mıṣr u Şām u Ḥalebi tesḫīr eyledi
ḥattā ḫādimüʾl-ḥaremeyniʾş-şerīfeyn elḳābını
ḫutbe-i laṭīfesinde teẕkīr ėtdi
lā siyyemā şāh *İsmāʿīl-i Erdebilī* gibi
ṣāḥib-ḫurūcuñ inhizāmına
ve Mıṣr sulṭānı *Ḳanṣu Ġavrī* gibi
bülend iḳtidāruñ ḳatl-i intiḳāmına
mücerred sekiz yılda
bu miḳdār fütūḥāt-i celīle ile
ʿāmme-i memālikūñ intiẓāmına
sāʿid-i müsāʿid-i himmetini teşmīr ėtdi
ammā *Süleymān Ḫān*
ki
ḳarn-i ʿāşirdeki şāhinşāh-i memālik-sitāndur
ʿidāletle ḳırḳ sekiz yıl salṭanat ėyledi
bir pādisāh-i Kisrā-sezā
ve yetmiş dört sene miḳdārı ʿömr-i ʿazīzle muʿammer olub
nėçe fetḥ ve nėçe ġazā ėyledi
ʿahd-i bāhirüʾs-saʿdındaki memālik-i maḥrūse sınurı
tā Baṣra ve Laḥsāya

1 tesḫīr: tesḫīr tesḫīr *L* | 6 ʿahd-i: ʿahdı *L*

ve Ḥabeşe ve Yemen gibi serḥadd-i müntehāya
müntehī idügini hüveydā èyledi
ve bi'l-cümle yigirmi beglerbegilik memleketlere
müstevlā olub
ṣanādīd-i 'ulemāya raġbet
ve ecāvīd-i şu'arāya ri'āyet
ve erbāb-i ḳaleme cüll-i himmet
ve aṣḥāb-i seyf-i muḥarreme küllī iltifāt u 'ināyet
ḳıldı
kaẕālik ferzend-i selīmü't-tab'-i mümtāz
ve ḫulḳ-i ṣāḥibü's-şeref-i lāzimü'l-i'zāzları
Selīm Ḫān
ki
cülūs-i taḫt-i salṭanatle kām-rān oldı
zamān-i devletleri
'ayş u maṣrūf olub
kendülere dāmād
ve ḫānedān-i mülk-i ma'muresine 'imād olan
vekīl-i a'zam-i celīlü'l-ḳadr-i nīkū-nihādları
Meḥemmed Paşa
hengām-i fırṣatda aḳrabā vu ta'alluḳātın ilerü çekmekle
ve nèçe nev-kīseleri ḳat'-i pāye ile
merātib-i sāmiyyeye naṣb ètmekle
niẓām-i 'ālem bir miḳdār iḫtilāle yüz ṭutdı
ve intiẓām-i aḥvāl-i benī Adem nev'an mütebeddil olub
nèçe ekābir ü ehālī ihāneti bezminüñ nevālesinden
kāse kāse zehirler yutdı
egerçeki şehriyār-i cihān
mūmā ileyh Selīm Ḫān
ḳānūn-i ḳadīme muḫālif evżā'a irḫā'-i 'inān
ètmezdi
ḥattā anuñ delāleti ile gāh u bī-gāh
ḫilāf-i himmet olan meẕāhibe bile
gitmezdi
lākin ol maḳūle dāmād
'ināyet-i mu'tād-i vizāret-i kübrā pāyesi ile
ḫānedān-i mülke 'imād olması
ve seḥergāh u şebāngāh
ol şehriyār-i Cem-gāh

8 raġbet: -ġbet *L*

neşāṭ-i keyfiyyet-i müdāmla mest-i maẖmūr bulunması
müşīr-i müşār ileyhüñ kemāl-i istıḳlāline
lā siyyemā dād-i istād vādīlerinde
'alā mā yürād ve taṣarrufātla kemā yebġī cāh u
celāline
sebeb olub
her ne 'arż ėylese muẖālefet ėylemezdi
(20) ve ba'ż-i maḥall olurdı ki
tevcīh eyledügi menāsibi 'arż u 'alāma daẖı mübāşeret
ėtmezdi
binā'en 'alā ẕālik
mizāc-i 'ālem-i mülk
ol devirdeki ẕemm-i fāsidle
münḥarif oldı
ve ḥumūżāt-i evżā'-i nā-hemvār
rūy-i gülgūnını zerd ėdüb
celb-i sīm ü zer sevdāsı
ve zamānenüñ ḥubb-i māl u menālle renc-i māliḥūlyāsı
ṣafravī marażlar ḥudūsı ile taġayyür buldı
taḥḳīḳ-i daḳīḳ ittifāḳ-i 'ukelā bile
(5b:1) devlet-i 'Oṣmāniyye kārẖāne-i mülk iẖtilāline
üç küfrānu'n-ni'metüñ birer vāki'a ilḳā'-i raẖnesi
sebeb olmışdur
ki
evvelki raẖne sulṭān Süleymāna dāmād olan *Rüstem Paşa*
mekri ile vāriṣ-i aḥaḳḳ-i mülk olan
*sulṭān Muṣṭafā-nām şehzāde*nüñ ḳatl ü ifnāsıdur
ikinci raẖne dāmād-i Selīm H̱ān olan sābiḳü'ẕ-ẕikr
Meḥemmed Paşa
kendü tevābi'ine menāṣıb-i 'āliyye
limūcibihī döndügi dād u sitād iḳtiżāsıdur
üçinci raẖne Rūmėli beglerbegiliginden müteṣā'id
(5) ve muṣāḥib-i şehriyārī namına baẖtı müsā'id
āl-i İsfendiyārdan *Şemsī Aḥmed Paşa*
sulṭān Murād H̱āna terġīb-i irtişā ėtdügi iżlāl u iġvāsıdur
felā cerem bu üç raẖne çār divār-i mülki
üç ṣadme ile mütezelzil ḳıldı
ve keṣret-i irtişā
šamsu'l-'aṣri kam yabqā 'alā šarafi'l-qaṣr feḥvāsınca

3 ikinci: iki *L* | 4& 8 döndügi: -öndügi *L* (?) |4 dād u sitād: dād sitād *L* | 7 Şemsī: Şems *L*

zevāl-i şems-i devletlerini
ḳarībü'l-'ahd döndügi gün gibi rūşen olub
emārāt-i üfūl u ġurūbuñ ṭulū' u ẓuhūrı
niẓām-i 'ālemi şekl-i āḫara müteḥavvil ėyledi
ve ol beyt-i ma'murı esāsına dek münhedim ü mużmaḥıl ḳıldı

li-münşī'ihī

'ālemüñ çun mizācı oldı saḳīm
vācib oldı ki ḥākim ola ḥakīm
līk ḥākim daḫı olundı marīż
marażuñ 'arzın añladı ta'rīż
oldı gitdükçe ol maraż mümtedd
nėçe mümtedd ziyāde ve müştedd
şerbet-i 'adl içürmeyince ṭabīb
nėçe ḳurtılsun ol saḳīm-i ġarīb
cem'-i māl özge renc-i hāyildür
māliḫūlyā 'ilācı müşkildür

neṡr egerçeki beyān olınduġı üzere āṡār-i evāyil -i iḫtilāl
sulṭān Selīm zamānında muḳarrer idi
ammā erbāb-i menāṣıbuñ derbeder olub
gezmeleri nā-mükerrer idi
ne ḥālse kitāb-i irtişā bir bāba derc olınmışdı
sükkān-i ḥarem-i a'lā
ve sāyir-i nüdemā
cidden ümūr-i mülke karışmazdı
ve esrār-i salṭanat u mülk içerüden ṭaşra çıḳub
efvāh-i 'avāmma düşmezdi
ḥattā ol 'aṣruñ şu'arāsından Mevlānā Fehmī
bu ḳıṭ'ayı demişidi
'arż-i ḥāl ṣūretinde yār-i büzürgvāra ṣunmışdı

ḳıṭ'a-i Fehmī

bir bildürür kimse yoġ aḥvāl-i 'ālemi
sulṭān-i dehr ḳaldı verā'-i ḥicābda

11 'arżın: 'arż *L* | 16 'avāmma düşmezdi: avāmma ve düşmezdi *L*

sercümle cem'-i māla muḳayyed vekīller
ammā ki nār-i faḳrla herkes 'aẕābda
müftī vü şeyḫ rāzı demez şāh-i 'āleme
bildür denilse ne ise der bunı yazmaz kitābda

el-ḳıṣṣa
tafṣīl-i ḳıṣṣadan ḥıṣṣa budur
ki
kibār-i selāṭīn-i selef
ve aḫyār-i ḫavāḳīn-i ṣāḥib-şeref
ki
gelüb geçmişlerdür
rūz-i ḥaşra dek nām-i bülendleri zinde
ve tavārīḫ-i muḫtelifetü'r-rivāyātla
serencām-i salṭanat-i fuḫrāları
ṣaḥāyif-i eyyām
ve ṣafāyiḥ-i şühūr u a'vāmda
bāḳī vü pāyende olmaġa
bā'is̱
ve meclis be-meclis teẕekkür olınduḳça
du'ā'-i ḫayırla rūḥ-i şerīfleri
şād ḳılınmaġa
bevā'is̱
(6a:1) zamān-i devletlerindeki
'ulemā'-i mü'ellifīnüñ taṣnīfāt u ās̱ārı
ve şu'arā'-i büleġā'-i belāġat-güzīnüñ muḳaṭṭa'āt u ḳaṣāyidle
naẓm-i ebrārıdur
ki
ḥikāyāt-i a'yān-i selefi yazmışlardur
aladdu'l-ašyā'i tilāvatu'aḫbāri'l-ḥukamā'i mażmūnına
iltifāt u raġbet göstermişlerdür
ol sebeble kendüler daḫı selīfine
ḫalīfe-i ṣāḥib- şeref olub
'afā'llāhu 'ammā salaf du'āsına
liyāḳat ḥāṣıl ėtmişlerdür
ve ol zümre-i ḥamīdeden mürşid-i aṣḥāb-i vera' u taḳvā
maḥbūb-i meşāyiḫ-i ẕevī'l-istihdā

3 kendüler daḫı: kendüler ve daḫı *L* | 6 futūḥı Edrenevī: 'l-l-futūḥı Edrenevrī *L*

vāṣıl-i ḥaḳḳ *ʿĀşıḳ Paşa bin Muḫlıṣ Paşa*
ve zümre-i müʾerrīḫinüñ rūḥ-i bā-futūḥı
Edrenevī *Mevlānā Rūḥī*
ve mütetebbiʿ-i ḳıṣaṣ u ās̱ār
Monlā Neşrī-i münteşir-güftār
ve müʾellif-i kitāb-i *Cāmiʿüʾl-meknūnāt* Mevlānā *ʿĪsā*-nām
Ḥamīdī-i ḥamīde-kirdār
ki
evvelā *Tevārīḫ-i āl-i ʿOs̱mānı* taḥrīr ėtmişler
sulṭān Bāyezīd Ḫān bin sulṭān Meḥemmed Ḫān ʿaṣrına dek
ẓuhūr ėden ḥavādis̱ ü ġarāyibini
naẓm u nes̱irle iḳtiżāʾ-i zamāna göre tesṭīr ėtmişler
eġerçeki kemā yalīḳ müʾellif ü münşī degül
ėdükleri maʿlūm
hele yazduḳları ḥavādis̱-i eyyām
anlaruñ taḥrīr ü ās̱ārı ile nā-mensī ve ġayr-i mektūmdur

li-münşiʾihī

ḳıldılar nām-i mülūkı iḥyā
raḥmetüʾllāhi ʿaleyhim cemʿiyyā

baʿdemā müʾerriḫ-i bī-naẓīr
müʾellif-i belāġat-semīr
ḥased-kerde-i İbn-i Es̱īr
revāc-bürde-i güftār-i İbn-i Cerīr
münşī *Monlā Īdrīs*-i şehīr
ki
Ebūʾl-fetḥ *sulṭān Meḥemmed* zamānında ḫāk-i Rūmı teşrīf
eyledi
anlaruñ fermān-i laṭīfleri ile
Tevārīḫ-i āl-i ʿOs̱mān teʾlīf ėyledi
ḥaḳḳan *Heşt bihişt*-nām
bir kitāb-i feṣāḥat-fercāmdur
ki
cā be-cā taʿaḳḳudü ġarābetinden ġayrī
ʿaybı yoḳdur

7 ve … Mevlānā: ve kitāb-i *Gāmi üʾl-meknūnāt*-i müʾellif-i Mevlānā *L* 8 Ḫān: Ḫān Ḫān *L*

ibhām u kināyāt
ve tevriye vü tecnīsāt
ve ta'biyesi me'mūl olan mertebelerden çoḳdur
tafāṣīl-i ḥikāyātı ḫod
gūyā ki
temāṣīl-i ṣunūf-i ḥurūfından artuḳdur
eger ehl-i Rūm fehmine aḳreb olsa nıẓrı muḥāl olurdı
aġreb-i kelimāt
'ālem-gīr edālar ile a'ẕeb olsa
me'āl-i imlāsı mūriṣ-i melāl olmaduġı ta'ayyün bulurdı
ḥattā ṣu'ūbetine binā'en ba'ż-i mevālī-i ehālī
(20) sulṭān Bāyezīd Ḫān bin Meḥemmed Ḫāna ilḳā ėtdiler
ol zamānda zümre-i müderrisīnden olan
Aḥmed bin Kemāl Paşa-i merḥūma
lisān-i Türkī ile taṣnīf ėtdürdiler
el-ḥaḳḳ ḫub yazmışlar
ol zamānda müsta'mel olan tibyān-i vāżıḥla beyān ėtmişler
vaḳtā ki sulṭā*n Süleymān Ḫān* zamānı oldı
müvaḳḳı'-i dīvān-i sulṭān
ṭuġrā-keş-i erkān-i ḫāḳānī
Celālzāde *mīr-i nişānī*
ki
nām-i laṭīfi Muṣṭafā
(6b:1) ve hem-nām-i sulṭān-i enbiyādur
Ṭabaḳātu'l-memālik-nām bir kitāb-i menşūr
te'līf eyledi
resm ü āyīn-i āl-i 'Osmān 'alā't-tertīb taṣnīf eyledi
ba'de müddetin müvakkı'-i dīvān
ve nişānī 'unvānı ile
'umde-i erkān olan
mīr Meḥemmed bin Ramażān
ki
anuñ manṣıbı ile müşār ileyhi bi'l-benān oldı
te'līf-i Tevārīḫ-i 'Osmānīyān
ḫiẕmet-i lāzime-i tuġrā-keşān olmak taṣavvurı ile
(5) bir kitāb daḫı anuñ reşeḥāt-i aḳlāmından
ẓuhūr u ṣudūr buldı
egerçeki evvel-i āferīnişden yazmışdur
ammā fihrist ṣūratı ile mücmelen taḥrīr ėdüb
bir risāle-i kebīr ḥacminde
itmāma ėrdürmişdür

ba'd ez ān
'ālim-i nādire-dān
fāżil-i sütūde-iẕ'ān
'umde-i müderrisīn-i dirāset-nişān
Mevlānā *Sa'du'd-dīn bin Ḥasan Cān*
bir sermed-ārāste-i ẕī şān
ve taḥrīr-i taḥrīrāne ile engüşt-nümāy-i a'yān iken
Tevārīḫ-i āl-i 'Oẕmān yazdılar
ḥaḳḳan ki lisān-i türkīde te'līf eyleyen eslāfa tefavvuḳ
ėdüb
sikkeyi mermerde ḳazdılar
hem edāsı rūḥ-efzā
ve inşāsı maṭbū' u dil-küsā
hem ḥikāyātı dil-ārā
ve basṭ-i müḳaddimātı maḳbūl u baḫşādur
ġıbbe ẕālik ümerā'-i rūzgār
cem'-i māla sālik ve vüzerā'-i büzürgvār
iddiḫār-i zer ü sīme mütehālik
ṣanādīd-i 'ulemā kemāl-i himmetle gūşe-i inzivāda
mebhūt
ecāvīd-i fużalā birer bucaḳda maḥzūn ve ṣāḥib-i sükūt
ve vā'iẓlerüñ pend ü naṣīḥati
ekābirüñ tabī'atlerine göre lāyiḥ
meşāyiḫüñ tekmīl-i ṭarīḳatı
berāy-i ma'āş idügi idügi rūşen ü vāẓıḥ olub
kibār u ṣiġār müzaḫrefāt-i dünyeviyye i'tibārında
eşrāf u aḫyār muḥassenāt-i dīniyye iḫtibārında
erḳām-i ma'ārifüñ defteri dürildi
aṣḥāb-i laṭāyifüñ muḥāsebātı ne ṭaleb ḳılındı
ne ṣorıldı

li-münşī'ihī

yėrinüb evrāḳını 'ilm ü 'ażruñ
indiler ṭāḳçe-i nisyāna
fużalā ṣadrına geçdi cühelā
raġbet ėtdi ulular nā-dāna

7 müderrisīn-i dirāset-nişān: müderrisīn ve dirāset-nişān *L*

eller üzre tutılan dürr ü güher
redd eliyle atılub yabāna
ẕillete düşdi ekābir cümle
çıḳdı bir bir süfehā meydāna

(20) çūnki aḥvāl-i rūzgār
bu minvāl ile āşkār oldı
sevād-ḫān mertebesindeki rū-siyehler
yüz aḳluġı da'vası ile hünerverler nāmına
vücūd buldı
evvelā *Loḳmān*-nām
inna mina'š-ši'r la-ḥikmatun mażmūnı fehminde nā-kām
naẓm u nes̱rüñ kemāl-i iẕ'ānında
noḳṣānı tamām
zümre-i ḳużātdan bir şaḫṣ-i nā-mevzūn kelām
baġteten şehnāmegūy-i ḫāḳānī oldı
(7a:1) ḥattā mü'ellifīn-i mü'erriḫīnden biri
zihī ḥikmet-i loḳmānī dėyü ol naẓm-i bī-niẓāmına
imżā daḫı urdı
der 'aḳb *Nuṭḳī*-nām bir ḥayvān-i nāṭıḳ
yine şehnāmegūylik rütbesine lāyıḳ görildi
hengāme-gīr şeyyādına
ve ḳiṣṣa-ḫān nāmına
bir rüsvāy-i māder-zād
ve 'acemīliği ile 'Acemlerden ma'dūd bir rūstā-yi bī-nihād
iken
mīr-i ṣadr-i şu'arā maḳāmı anuñ gibi erẕeli iclāsla
mükedder ḳılındı
(5) ba'demā *aš-šay' lā yuṯannā illā wa qad yuṯallaṯ* mıṣdāḳınca
İbn-i Ta'līḳī Meḥemmed Çelebī-nām
bir maḥmūdü 'l-eṭvār-i be-nām ile
şehnāmeguylik rütbesi müs̱elles̱ ḳılınub
ol maḫdūm-i nebālet-nişān
şehnāmegūy olmaḳ sa'ādeti ile meşhūr-i cihān oldı
ḥālā ki üç nām-dāruñ ikisi
evc-i hevā-yi hevesde zāġ u zaġan gibi perān
ve berāy-i iẓhār-i 'irfān
bāzār-i āzār-i 'ālemiyānda
bir ḳuzġun-nāme iştirāsına ḳizġun müşterī idükleri meyyān

3 rūstā-yi: rūstā *L* | 5 maḥmūd: maḥmūde *L*

ve deh mürġ ḳiṣṣası fehmine
ʿadem-i ḳudret ü biżāʿaları nümāyān
kec-fehm ü bī-iẕʿān idükleri
ʿāmme-i ḫavāṣṣ ve kāffe-i ʿavāmm miyānında
taʿayyün
ancaḳ Taʿlīḳīzāde neẓer ü ḫoş-ḫirām gibi
naẓm u nes̱r yazısında kendüsini cilve-i ber-āmāda uyarub
cürmüñ havāsında bāl u perr-i iḳtidārını küşāde gösterdi

li-münşīʾihī

ʿuluvv-i mertebeden pādişāh-i ʿālem-gīr
meger ki ėtmedi anlara iltifāt-i yesīr
taṣavvur eyledi her biri naẓma ḳādir ola
edā-yi pākla inşāda belki māhir ola
anuñçün oldı muḳārin riżā-yi sulṭānī
nėçe riʿāyet ü iḥsāni gördi erzānī
ikisi gerçe mükerrem zaʿīm-i vaḳt oldı
nihāyet arada Nuṭḳī ẓemīm-i vaḳt oldı
ol ikisine verildi yarar zeʿāmetler
olındı sözlerine iltifāt ve raġbetler

nes̱r muḥaṣṣal-i kelām
sulṭān Selīm Ḫān-i Cem-cām
meclis-i salṭanatinde neşʾeʾ-i devletle ḳıyām ėtdügi eyyām
reʾīs-i küttāb olan mīr Ferīdūn bin ʿAbduʾl-Celīl
ki
ṣadr-i aʿẓam olan Meḥemmed Paşa-i ṭavīl
ḫiẕmetindeki esrāra maḳrūn
küllü kātibin taʿrīfi ile biżāʿası rūz-efzūn
bir şaḫs-i muḫterem idi
mezbūr Loḳmānı paşasına ḥüsn-i terbiyet ḳıldı
ol dahı gerçek ṣanub
şehnāmegūy olmasını münāsib gördi
kużāt-i ḳaṣabāt miyānındaki mercūḥlardan iken
aʿazz zeʿāmetle naẓm-i kelāma meʾmūr oldı
pes mezbūr sulṭān Selīmüñ ferzend-i reşīdi
sulṭān Murād Ḫān-i kerīmüñ zamān-i salṭanatlarında bulduġın
naẓm ėyledi

(7b:1) üstād-i büleġā olan Firdevsī-i Ṭūsī
'ālem-i rūḥānīde nėçe rūzgār
mezbūruñ zehr-āb-i taḳlīd ü tetebbu'ını hażm eyledi
ḥālā ki rūḥ-i ḥakīm bir 'aẕāb-i elīm belāsına daḫı giriftār
oldı
ya'nī ki meẕkūr Nuṭḳī-i 'acemīnüñ şehnāmegūy olması ile
ḥüzn ü endūhı bir iken hezār
vaḳtī ki ol ḫiẕmet-i ḫāṣṣ giderek Ta'līḳīzādeye daḫı iḫtiṣāṣ
buldı
naẓm-i kelāma ḳādir olanlaruñ üç rütbeleri
bil-külliyye ḥażīż ü pest olmayub
nev'an tesliyet bulmaları ta'ayyün buldı
zīrā ki beyne'l-'ulemā dūdmān-i büzürgvār añılan
āl-i Fenārī baḳiyyesi
bir maḫdūm-i 'āḳıl ve bīgāne-i bī-mümās̱il idügi
kitābında beyān olınmışdur
ya'nī ki manẓūme-i Tārīḫ-i āl-i 'Os̱mānī dibācesinde
bu ebyātla vaṣf-i ḥālin bildürmişdür

naẓmuhū

atam ve dedem menziline vuṣūl
müyesser ola dėyü tā ki ḥuṣūl
varub şeh Murād-i civān devlete
erem dėyü ben nā-tüvān devlete
kütübden nėçe tercüme ėyledüm
nėçe sinn daḫı gitdürem söyledüm
bu ḥāl üzre devretdi cebr-i bülend
cülūs-i hümāyūn olub ercümend
beni şāha şehnāmegūy ėtdiler
tenem mūyeden līk mūy ėtdiler

'alā küllī ḥāl
bu iki naẓm-gūy-i memdūḥu'l-maḳāl
'ālem-i naẓmuñ niẓāmına revāc verdiler
memdūḥları olan selāṭīn-i 'iẓāmuñ
evṣāf-i ḥasenesine kūşiş ḳıldılar

pes mezbūr monlā Loḳmānuñ zebān-i farsīde vāḳıʿ olan ebyātdan
bir ḳaç beyt
ve lisān-i türkīdeki naẓmında
Taʿlīḳīzādeye muʿāraża yüzinden söyledüği ḳıtʿa
bu maḥallde īrād olınmışdur
ki kemāl-i belāġatı ve ẕū'l-lisān olduġı ḳudreti
bunlardan künhi ile maʿlūmdur

naẓmuhū fī lisāni'd-derī

be-haftād-u panč az ṣad-i haštumīn
be-durğ-i šah uftād durr-i ṯamīn
yakī qaṭra az baḥr-i nīsān-i ʿilm
be-qudrat šude ʿayn-i insān-i ʿilm
be-sar tāğ-i šāhī vu hast-i salīm
be-ḥikmat ṭalab-gār-i fayḍ-i ḥakīm
ğulūsiš nuhṣad-u hağdah be-kām
be-u luṭf-i ḥaqq yār-u hamrah mudām
musaḫḫar namūd az ʿArab tā ʿAğam
be-iqlīm-i ʿOṯmān befarsūd ṣanam

ve naẓmuhū fī türkī

ʿaceb fikr ėylemiş Taʿlīḳīzāde
dėye şehnāme maḫdūm-i mükerrem
eger Türkīdür ise ḳıṣṣa maʿlūm
veñilüb Farsīden urıcaḳ dem
aġır yükdür nola hempā olursa
ḥarf-i cemālī ile bir ḳaç adım

bunlardan maʿādā
sulṭān Murād Ḫān vaṣfındaki Şemāyil-nāme-nām kitābında
terġīb-i rezmle dėmişdür ki

15 ẕū: ẕ *L* | 18 ğulūsiš: ğulūs *L* | 19 be-iqlīm: bā qalam *L* | befarsūd: befarmūd *L*

naẓmuhū

dėmidür şehā sāz-i rezm ėdelüm
'adūv def'ına 'azm-i cezm ėdelüm
alub mülk-i İrānı başdan başa
ḳılub naṣīb o yėrlerde mīr u paşa
Timur ėllerin ėdelüm tār u mār
(8a:1) ḳoyalum cihān içre ḫoş yādigār
Timur Leng yıḳdıysa cāmi'leri
yapalum anuñ yıḳduġı yėrleri
eġer aldı İslāmdan ol esīr
biz āzād ėdelüm ṣaġīr ü kebīr
kimüñ kim tebarı sitemger ola
Timur gibi her çend server ola
yılan yavrısı gibi şeh-mār olur
ṣouḳ yüzlü pür-zehr ü mürdār olur

el-ḳıṣṣa Ta'līḳīzāde
ġıll u ġışş ḳaydından āzāde
levḥ-i ẕihni āyīne gibi jeng-i 'alāyıḳdan sāde
bir ferzāne-i
yegānedür
ki
ol birleri gibi ḫalṭ-i kelām ėtmeyüb
naẓm u neṡr birbirinden mümtāzdur
inşā-yi bedā-yi nişānınuñ ḫod sec'-i laṭīfi
ṣaḥīḥ ü mütebāyin olduḳdan ġayrī siyāḳ u sibāḳı mażbūṭ
semt-i merġūbla ḳıṣṣa-perdāz ḫuṣūṣā ki 'uluvv-i dergāh-i
vālā-sīmādan ziyāde sümūk-i müsteṡnādur dėyü
bu üç beyti ḫub naẓm ėtmişdür
hażm-i naḳṣ ėdüb
bu maḥallde ekābir-i selef ṭarīḳine gitmişdür

nagūyad kasī bartar ast āsmān
magar bāz našināsad az rīsmān
magar nā-šinās ast yā ğāhil ast
wayāḫud ču man ablah wa ġāfil ast
ki gūyad čenīn dīde'am dar kitāb
ki az māh rūšantar ast āfitāb

4 ḳaydından: ḳaydıdan *L* | 9 rīsmān: rīsmā *L*

ġibbe ẕālik pādişāh-i cihān
fermān-gāh-i kihān u mihān
sulṭān Meḥemmed Ḫān ibn-i sulṭān Murād Ḫān ile
Egri ḳalʿası fetḥine ḍoġrılub
baʿdeʾl-fetḥi veʾt-tesḫīr
naẓm-i Türkī nāmına tesṭīr ėyledüġi ebyāt-i lā-naẓīrden
bir ḳaç beytüñ īrādı münāsib görildi
yaʿnī ki biżāʿaʾ-i bī-iżāʿasını ibhāman bu maḥallde
naḳl u tesvīdine cürʾet olındı

dar madḥ-i monlāyān-i ʿaṣr gufte

nėçe Türk-i ḫar-ṭabʿ-i hīzem-şikāf
sezāvār-i pālān ḥarī-i ikāf
kitābini dīvāra mānend-i ḫişt
yıġar birbiri üzre ol bed-siriṣt
maʿānī oḳurılmayub resmini
ṣorarsañ azar fiʿli ḥarf ismini
eger baḥṣ-i ṭıbb olsa ġamdan olur
ṣorarsañ eġer küfri dinden olur
ammā ḥaḳḳ ki buṭlānı ẓāhir iken
fesādı çū bū çil bāhir iken
bulur manṣıbını dāyim ol bed-aṣıl
çu mefʿūl manṣūb olur muttaṣıl
saçaḳlu ʿabāyiye olur süvār
ki aña şerrābe aṣar rūzigār

dar ḫud-furūšī wu ḏikr-i šāhān saʾuḥyīhim tasʾālan lī mīsufte

muḥīṭ-i hüner baḥr-i ṭāmmī menem
ki çun cürʿa-peymāy-i cāmī menem
bu bī-devlet oldı çu devlet-sitā
ve bī-mār-i ġam ėtdi ḳadm-i dü-tā
ferāzende-i ḳadr-i şāhān menem
sitāyende-i Cem-külāhān menem
şecāʿat-sitā naḫl-bend-i şehān
zemīn-sāy-i süm-i semend-i şehān

13 lā-naẓīrden: la-naẓırdan *L* | 17 eger: ezer *L* | küfri dīnden: dīnden küfr *L*

alub āl-i Selcuḳı seyl-i fenā
olur nesl-i ʿAbbās-i ʿabūs ʿanā
ḳanı ʿizz-i Bū(viy)yān-i maḥmūd-ḫūy
ḳanı Ṭāhirīyān-i pākīze-gūy
(margin) ḳanı āl-i Ṣaffār-i āhen-güdāz
ḳanı Serbedārān-i gerden-firāz
ḳılubdur Süleymān-i ṣāḥib-ḫadem
rehīn-i fenāda rehīn-i ʿadem
tevārīḫ ʿilminden oldur mürād
ki maʿlūm ola Rüstem ü Keyḳubād
(8b:1) laḳab-nāme-i defter-i Keyḳubād
varaḳ ber varaḳ oldı ber-bād-i yād
oḳunsa eger dīv-i pülādvend
ḫüdāvend-i kūpāl u gürz ü kemend
eger olsa meẕkūr Ekvān-dīv
bėl-i nerre-dīvān güneh-kān ḫıdīv
Demāvend ḍaġında behīme ṣanur
Ḫazer deşti içinde ḫayme ṣanur
yabānda Siyāvuḫşı vaḫşı sezer
eger resmimi görse Raḫşı sezer

neẕr eġerçeki kitābındaki ebyāt
birbirinden aʿlā nėçe bunuñ gibi vāridātdur
lākin iżāʿa-i evkāt ḫāṭırasından
bu miḳdārla iktifā maḥż-i dil-nüvāzī
ve ʿarż-i iltifātdur
ʿalāʾl-ḫuṣūṣ fārsī naẓımları daḫı vardur
ekẕeri maḳbūl u laṭīf ü ebrārdur
ve her birindeki taṣarrufāt-i ḫāṣṣaları bi-şümārdur
maʿa ẕālik cümlesi pesend ü maḥabbete lāyıḳ ve sezāvārdur
ammā Mevlānā Nuṭḳī miʿyār-i imtiḥāna dāḫil
ve ḫar-mühre-i kelāmı
anlaruñ cevāhir-i nādirüʾn-niżāmı ile
maḥall-i ʿarża vāṣıl
olmaḳ lāzim geldükde
bedīʿ ḳıṣṣası naḳlini naṣm-i bedīʿüʾl-beyān menzilesine
tenzīl ėtmişdür
ḥaḳḳā kim
rindāne ve pür-tövb sābıḳı gibi

2 dīvān: īvān *L*

nazm u nesre müteʿallık olan ʿuyūbını açmamışdur
el-kıṣṣa gördüm ki
aḥvāl-i ʿālem her cihetle vājgūn
ṣāḥib-i ṣadr olan ekābir-i ümem ḥubb-i dünyā ile
memkūr u meftūn
sinīn-i sinnim ise
isney ve ḫamsīnden füzūn *er-raḥīl sümme'r-raḥīl* ṣadāları ise
ānan ve ānan ṣımāḫ-i semʿime maḳrūn
hemānā ki tereşşüh-i emṭār-i sübḥanī yüzi suyına
ḫāb ġafletinden göz açdum
kendü kendüme pend ėdüb
bu ebyāt-i cevāhir-nisār maẓmūnıyla ḫāksār ḫılḳatıma
güherler saçdum

nazm

ay ki pangāh raft dar ḫᵛābī
magar īn panč rūz dard yābī
kay namāz-i nuw mustaǧāb šavad

nazm

kay be-yak rūy dar du miḥrābī

felā cerem müstaʿīnen min müfīżi'l-ḥikem ve zaḫr-i āḫiret
içün
kitāb-i *Künhü'l-aḫbār* te'līfine el urdum
müslimīn-i müteʿaṭṭışīne zülāl-i ʿırfān ifādesini
münāsib gördüm
tā ki mücelledāt-i çār
ki dördincisi tevārīḫ-i āl-i ʿOsmān ḥavādisini iḫbārdur
ṣāniʿ-i āmürzgārdan istiʿānetle taḥrīrini encāma ėrgürdüm
ümidvārum ki
ḥażret-i kirdigār *celle şa'nuhū ʿane'l-iẓhāri ve'l-iżmār*
ol mücelledāt-i çihār

15 dar yābī: dard be-ābī *L* | kay: ki *L*

kemāl-i raġbet ü i'tibārla
rub'-i meskūnı devvār
ve eḳālīm-i seb'ayı seyyār ola
ḫuṣūṣan iştihār-i nüsḫa-i büzürgvār
şeyḫ Sa'dīnüñ Gülistānı
ve Mevlānā Cāmīnüñ Bahāristānı gibi ḫazān u bahār
ve leyālī vü nehār
şöhre-i ḫıredmendān-i rūzgār
ve mā bihī'l-iftiḫār-i debīrān-i hüner-kirdār idügi
muḥaḳḳaḳ ola
tā ki vālidīn-i marḥūmīn-i ġufrān-dis̱ār
ve ḫavānīn-i maḫdūmīn-i 'irfān-şi'ār
ḫuṣūṣan bu kitābuñ müsevvedātı
beyāżına kūşiş-i bī-şümār eden semīy-i resūl-i kirdigār
feyżı muḫlıṣ ve Meḥemmed-nām olan birāder-i fermān-berdār-i
sa'ādetvār bile
(9a:1) berḫurdār olub
mü'ellif-i mücrim ü günehkār
ve muṣannıf-i müte'essif-i perişān-efkār
dünyā vu āḫiret sa'ādetlerinden ṭūl-i 'ömürle maḳżī'l-evṭār
ve meclis be-meclis-i ẕikr-i cemīl
ve du'āy-i bī-'adīl
ve ecr-i cezīl mezāyāsından
behredār ḳılınması
taḥaḳḳuḳ u ta'ayyun bula
ḥażret-i ḫüdāy-i büzürgvār
'ālim ve vāḳıf-i esrārdur
ki
bu te'līfden murādum temeṭṭu'-i menāfi'-dis̱ār
ve tevaḳḳu'-i dirhem ü dīnār degüldür
zīrā ki
agāh u ḫaberdārum ki
cemī'-i kār u bār
ve raġbet-i 'ırż u nāmūs u veḳār
ve devlet-i dünyāya müte'allıḳ olan ṭumṭurāḳ u ās̱ār
mānend-i 'ömr-i 'ācil
ẓıll-i zāyildür

23 -berdār: birāder *L* | bile: tile *L* | 1 mü'ellif-i mücrim *D*: mü'ellif ü mücrim *L* | 2 maḳżī *L*: tefaṣṣī *D* | 3 'ālim ve vāḳıf-i *L*: 'ālim-i vāḳıf-i *D* | 5 'ırż u nāmūs *L*: 'ırż-i nāmūs *D* | 6 ẓıll-i *D*: ve ẓıll-i *L* | göñlümde *D*: göñlinde *L*

li-münşī'ihī

işbu te'līfden budur maḳṣūd
ola göñlümde ḥuzn u ġam mefḳūd
her murādum ḫüdā ʿināyet ėde
ḳılmayım ėllere rükūʿ u sücūd
ṭūl-i ʿömr ü kemāl-i ʿilm ü ʿamel
ḫalef-i ṣāliḥ ü ṣalāḥ-i vücūd
ṣıdḳıyla tövbe ḫayr-i ḫātime hem
şükr-i memdūd ve menzil-i maḥmūd
baña rūzī ḳılub ėde mevlā
seyyi'ātum varaḳların nā-būd
çekmeyim ḫavf-i cisr ü mīzānı
(10) ola ben bendeden ḫüdā ḫoşnūd
görmeyim nār-i dūzaḫuñ şererin
gözüme girmeye ol oddan dūd
cennet içre maḳām-i maḥmūdum
dār-i dünyāda ḳıl baña meşhūd
tāziyān ėtmeyim taṣavvurdan
çārsūy-i ʿamelde germ ola sūd
yā ilāhī be-ḥaḳḳ-i ṣınf-i ümem
yā ilāhī be-ḥaḳḳ-i her mevcūd
ya'nī her milletüñ du'ası ile
(13) baña ḳıl luṭf-i vücūd nā-maʿdūd

11 maḥmūdum *L*: maḥmūdı *D*

TRANSLATION OF THE PREFACE

(3a:15) *About the reasons for writing this book and the motive for its pleasant composition; it means to explain the praiseworthy personal merits and ancestral distinction of the kings of the Keeper of the World (i.e. God) belonging to the dynasty of ʿOs̱mān; it intends to throw light on the establishment of this Family of Holy War, which occurred between the year 700 of the Hijra (1300/01) and the year 1006 (1597/98); it will recount, then, the appearance and consolidation of one generation after another of the kings of the surrounding regions who were their contemporaries, and describe the way in which their rule was established in the capitals of their countries; it will, furthermore, summarily describe the works and books written by some groups of those* ʿulemā *who were favored by their excellent protection, and disclose these events in a concise way.*

(20) The swimmer in the sea overflowing with ink, who is a diver in the ocean of divine inspiration and assistance, has always brought, it seems, jewels of sudden thought to the surface from the mother-of-pearl of inkpot and pen-and-ink-case, and has always offered ready money on the market of good repute where business is brisk, and in the street of creditable bankers and moneylenders. The traveller through cities and large towns of black ink, who finds himself in the valley where the right path is followed and the proper thing is done, and who visits the
(3b:1) regions of light, thought and intellect, has always, as is reported, procured rare drops of the water of life from the darkness beyond the ocean and the inky compounds of the fathomless depth, and has always been ready to string a necklace of pearls for the cultivators of talent of house and home (i.e. his country) and the instigators of wisdom of all times and ages.

[*A poem*] *by the author*

With his black turban he became a ʿAbbāsid
every reed-pen before him turned black ink (lit. 'blackness') into a fair copy (lit. 'whiteness')
On his tongue lies, folded up, his language; on his head (he wears) clearly visible his shawl,
and in his hands he always holds his staff: so it is for the omniscient Philosopher
But he has spoken from heart and soul,
and his poetry and prose result from these two tongues.

If his tinder-burner had been full of unrefined ambergris,
(5) he would have started to perfume the brains of the crowds.
But this fruit-yielding date-palm is a pen
that goes about among immature mankind.

He (i.e. the author) spelled out the brilliant meanings [of this book]—and this induced him to write [it in the first place]—and wrote down its heart-rending contents—and this you might reckon a further motive for recording these chapters — in such a way as the well-known stories, high and low, and however humble and noble, [composed] until the year thousand according to the approved era counted from the Hijra (1591/92) had become thoroughly familiar to the inhabitants of the dusty countries and the members of the heavenly congregation
(margin) (i.e. the death) through the [traditional] histories and works of the historians of Rūm (i.e. the Ottoman Empire), subtle and learned minds who each, individually, had been authorities of laws and customs (*ḳavānīn ü rüsūm*) in the lofty ranks of the *ʿilmīye* in compliance with the saying "each of us has his appointed place"[1], and who had plucked the first fruits of their pure intelligence from the for-ever fruit-bearing trees in the garden where the fruit of scholarship especially matures by
(8) traditional knowledge, stories which regard, in particular, the identity of the sultans passing over the surface of the earth, and the rulers of the cultivated kingdoms,
(10) i.e. the sovereigns who have been sitting on their thrones, the so-called 'Masters of Sermon and Coin', as well as the creed and religion, order and customs, and commands and laws by which they have become famous, from the region of Rūm, full of possibilities, up to the frontiers of India, Cathay and China.

According to the correct procedure [outlined above, I might say] that the pick of the Ottomans and 'Masters of Crown and Mint' who sat on the throne in their Capital Constantinople, was Sultan Murād Ḫān, son of Sultan Selīm Ḫān, who has attained mercy (i.e. has died)[2]. He was the twelfth successful and happy ruler in the eminent chain of august sovereigns who have been Lords of the World since 300 years[3].

(15) [Proceeding] in the same way, it was Shah ʿAbbās who sat on the throne of Qazwīn, a ruler who occupied the highest place honour in the populous dominions of Persia. He was the son of Ḫudābanda, son of Shah Ṭahmāsb who has chosen departure for another place of abode (i.e. died)[4] and was the seventh Chosraw[5]

[1] Koran, sura 37:63.
[2] I.e. Sultan Murād III (1574-1595). His predecessor Sultan Selīm II died in 1574.
[3] The dynasty was politically established by ʿOs̱mān *Ġāzī* (1281-1324) in western Anatolia.
[4] I.e. Shah ʿAbbās I (1588-1629). His grand-father, Shah Ṭahmāsb, died in 1576.
[5] The name of several Sassanid kings, and also of one of the heroes of the *Šāhnāma* ('The Book of Kings') of Firdawsī.

on the throne of the elevated dynasty of the shahs of Ardabil who have reigned for almost 100 years[6].

After him, it was ʿAbdullāh Ḫān, son of Iskender Ḫān[7] who ruled over the Kingdom of Bukhārā and sat on the highest place of honour, the throne of Samarqand. He was 'Master of the Royal Cypher' and Uzbekian king, the twelfth sovereign[8] who conformed to canon law and was strong in his religion in the line of the
(20) powerful king, known by the name of ʿAbulḫayr Oġlan, a *ṣāḥib-żuhūr* ('one who raises himself to power and dominion')[9], who ruled 150 years ago.

By far the most renowned king of India, and to be specific, the fifth celebrated ruler and offspring of *ṣāḥib-ẓuhūr* Timur, indeed, was Jalāluddīn[10], the son of Sultan Humāyūn. He has been the greatest (*Akbar*), and most victorious [prince]
(4a:1) among the Rajahs of India, and was altogether one of the most famous and prominent padishahs through his perfect munificence and generosity, freely expending on gifts and presents.

Apart from them, it was Sherīf Ḥasan, son of Abū Numayy, who was sherīf and prince of Mecca the Honorable and endowed with a sound and celebrated pedigree and pure and most renowned personal qualities. From 400 years ago until the year 1000, the rule [of his family] has not been challenged, and his Sermon and Mint has made up his fame in house and home (i.e. in his country). He was the 27th [descendant] of the family of Ṭāhā and Yāsīn and the lofty offspring of the best of Apostles (i.e. Muḥammad)[11], who occupied his high office with his glorious seal.

[6] These shahs belonged to the Ṣafavid dynasty, which ruled Iran from Shah Ismāʿīl I (1501-1524). Shah ʿAbbās I was actually the fifth ruling shah in succession. The dynasty which started as a *ṣūfī ṭarīḳat*, was established by Sayḫ Safīʾd-dīn (d. 1334) in Ardabil in Azerbayjan.

[7] I.e. ʿAbdullāh II (1583-1598) belonging to the dynasty of the Shaybānids, who ruled Transoxania.

[8] ʿAbdullāh II was in fact the eleventh Uzbekian ruler since Abūʾl-ḫayr (1429-1468).

[9] A ruler of this title could legitimate his authority in the Muslim world on the grounds of his successful if unexpected expansion of his power, which was apparently sanctioned by God. ʿOs̱mān *Ġāzī* was also considered to be one of them, cf. Fleischer, 'Âlî', 509.

[10] I.e. Jalāluʾd-dīn Akbar I (1556-1605). He was actually the third Moghul Emperor who ruled India since Bābūr (1526-1530). Bābūr was separated from Timur by five generations on his father,s side.

[11] This was Ḥasan b. Abī Numayy (1553/54-1607/08), cf. İ. H. Uzunçarşılı, *Mekke-i Mükerreme emirleri* (Ankara 1972), in: *Türk Tarih Kurumu Yayınları* VII 59, 77. He was actually the 33th sherif in line since ʿAbduʾl-ʿazīz Qatāda, the founder of the dynasty, who ruled ca. 1203/04, cf. E. de Zambaur, *Manuel de généalogie et de chronologie pour l'histoire de l'Islam* (Hannover 1927), 21-22, so, indeed, 400 years before. The two groups of mystical letters ṭāhā (ṭ, h) and yāsīn (y, s) are the title of subs. the 20th and 36th chapters of the Koran and are considered by some interpreters to be names of the Prophet. The 'family of Ṭāhā and Yāsīn' stands thus also for the family of Muḥammad. ʿĀlī knew sherif Ḥasan personally and showed him his *Mevāʿid* in Mecca in 1599/1600, cf. Fleischer, 'Âlî', 333.

(5) It was, however, Ġāzī Giray Ḥassān, son of Devlet-Giray Ḫān, khan in the capital
city of the Crimea, the fortunate and glorious offspring of the family of Chingiz
and one of those who had their place among the Tatar rulers of noble descent,
kings of exalted lineage. He was the 26th khan since the praised Ḥāccī Ḫān,
(margin) who ruled from the year 854 AH (1450/51) onwards, had come to the fore,
and a mighty ruler endowed with the magnificence of his background. He was,
moreover, the 11th *ġazā*-waging and land-conquering sovereign since Mengli Ḫān,
(7) who is included in the column of 26 khans[12].

Although the famous Khan we mentioned, and the illustrious possessor of titles
who is called the sherīf of Mecca the Honourable, are both renowned by their
Mint and Sermon, and celebrated men who expand their territories, it is clear
that they have presented their respectful service to the sultans of the House of
(10) ʿOs̱mān and are mentioned after the Ottoman kings in the recitation of the sermon
of sublime degree[13]. They have been accustomed to unfold their banners (i.e. of
the Ottomans) and have been obedient to their exalted orders, and although they
bowed their heads to their noble authorisations (i.e. of the Ottoman Sultans),
they, nevertheless, have been two strongwilled rulers who command respect.

All the same it is, for sure, clear and evident that the shah of Persia and the khaqan of the Turks who exert a powerful influence, send complimentary letters at every turn, and persistently offer their respect and love [to the Ottomans].

A peculiar case, however, is Jalāluddīn who is deprived of this honour, because
(15) the long distance has been considered an impediment for the exchanging of
ambassadors, but there is proof that he offered his apologies[14].

[12] Ġāzī Giray (1596-1608, second period of government) was the 20th Khan of the Crimea since Ḥāccī Giray who ascended on the throne in 1426 (not in 1450/51 as ʿĀlī thought), and was indeed the 11th Khan since Mengli ḳān, if one starts counting from his third period of government (1478-1514). See: C. E. Bosworth, *The Islamic Dynasties* (Edinburgh 1980, second impression), 157. The Giray Khans were descendants of Jochi, the eldest son of Chingiz Khan.

[13] The Girays were the traditional allies of the Ottomans against the Golden Horde and later the Russians. A formal dependance on Istanbul was shown by the requirement of a Giray hostage at the Ottoman Court. After the defeat of the Mamlūk sultans in 1516 by Selīm I, the sherif of Mecca submitted to the Ottomans in 1517, and the sultans became protectors of the two holy cities, Mecca and Medina.

[14] There never existed a regular diplomatic contact between the Ottomans and the Moghul Emperors, although the Uzbekian ruler ʿAbduʾllāh Khan tried to form a tripartite alliance against Safavid Persia. Jalāluʾd-dīn indeed tried to establish friendly relations with the Porte in 1556, when he sent a letter, by way of a shipwrecked Ottoman subject, to the sultan, in which he expressed his hope that 'friendship and unity' would come to exist between the two rulers, cf. A. Reshid, 'Ottoman-Mughul Relations during the seventeenth Century', in: *VI. Türk Tarih Kongresi (1961)*; *Kongreye sunulan bildiriler* (Ankara 1967), 536-544.

We all know now, moreover, from recorded history, that it is only necessary to attain importance to the sultans of the people of Islam, i.e. to the above mentioned powerful emperors, and that the doomed unbelievers, the so-called tribute-payers to the Sublime Threshold, i.e., the Spanish, French, the Pope of Rome, the Lutherans, the ʿAndī[15] of Georgia, the Circassians and Mingrelia, Transylvania, Walachia, the Ukraine (*Rus*), Moldavia, the Poles, Bohemians and Russia under the Czar (*Çar*), Hungary and the Germans, always were prepared to jump up and crawl on all fours to present their humble service in submission to the Shah of the Humā[16].

(20) *[A poem] by the author*

God made the sovereigns of the House of ʿO̱smān
    Servitors of the two sacred Fanes (i.e. Mecca and Medina).
If they had wished honour and glory for their country,
    they would have taken it like the Double-horned One[17].
If they had incited rebels,
    they would have obeyed and stood to attention.
Their swords' water flows over the earth,
    nobody is able to intervene with them.
If he is not trodden underfoot on their road,
    with how much disgrace a man of good repute will be confronted!
It is a religious duty to offer your soul exemplarily,
    one might consider it a debt to be paid off
(4b:1) A man who humbly prostates himself on the soil of the Court,
    directs his most perfect eyes to the comliest side[18].

The story.

During the reign of the well known and praised kings of the House of ʿO̱smān, i.e.: ʿO̱smān Ḫān the 'Ruler' (*Dāver*), Murād Ḫān, Yıldırım ('Thunderbolt') Bāyezīd Ḫān, Sultan Meḥmed Ḫān, Sultan Murād Ḫan, Sultan Meḥmed Ḫān the 'Conqueror', and especially the 'Generous' Sultan Bāyezīd Ḫān, the 'Conqueror

[15] This name refers to a region in the Caucasus and a river of the same name, see: M.F. Kırzıoglu, *Osmanlılar'ın Kafkaselleri'ni fethi (1451-1590)* (Ankara 1976), map 1.
[16] This was a mythical bird of happy omen, prognosticating a crown to every head it overshadowed and was especially associated with the Ottoman sultans.
[17] I.e. Iskender or Alexander the Great. He was, with Chingiz Khan and Timur, considered a *ṣāḥib-ḳırān*, a world-conqueror who establishes dominion of the earth, cf. Fleischer, 'Âlî', 508. No Ottoman sultan could as yet claim this title.
[18] The metre of the first hemistich of this *beyt* is irrigular, and the meaning of this couplet is not quite clear to me.

of Egypt' Sultan Selīm Ḫān, his fortunate and righteous son Sultan Süleymān Ḫān, the excellent son of his palace Selīm Ḫān, as well as the successor of His Majesty Sultan Murād Ḫān [19], the whole country of Rūm, as well as its dominions with their spacious coasts, which are the pride of this land, and its provinces (*vilāyet*s) resembling principalities (*eyālet*s), such as the largest part of the populous country of the Arabs, and the whole of Egypt, Syria and Aleppo, and especially the sacred cities [of Mecca and Medina], the regions of Yaṯrib and Baṭḥā [20], and those of Yemen, Aden, Abyssinia, Basra and Laḥsā [21], and—not to forget—the 'Island of the Kurds': Mosul and Diyarbekr, and Arabian Irak, Azerbayjān, Shirwān and all towns and capitals of Georgia, Mingrelia and Daghistān, and with these, the *eyālet*s of Algiers, La Golette, Tunis, Tripolitania, Cyprus and Rhodes, were, from beginning to end, and with all the annexes and dependencies under their jurisdiction, taken into their possession, concatenated in their illustrious chain by links of conquest and subjection, while their princes and potentates were sentenced and tied, one after another, and seized and overmastered by their crushing power.

Thus, in the year 1000, it was a fact that the dominions under the authority of the sultan called Murād III, a sublime victor of armies, who had satisfied his appetite in the twelfth womb, and a great monarch shining with universe-conquering and light-enhancing luck, comprised 40 *beglerbegilik*s and counted more than 300 *sancakbegi*s, while his great ancestor ʿOsmān Ḫān had only ruled over one province one might consider as the *beglerbegilik* of Anatolia.

When one comes to the age of Yıldırım Bāyezīd Ḫān [22], of the fourth generation, who ate his fill of intrigues against *ṣāḥib-ẓuhūr* Timur, one clearly sees that the dominions under his rule were extended to Karaman and Rūm [23], as well as to the countries to be described as the *beglik* of the *beg*s of Rumeli.

But the seventh noble offspring, Sultan Meḥmed Ḫān [24], the conqueror of countries and subjugator of Constantinople, extended the conquest of Rumeli to the border of Bosnia, and expanded Anatolia up to the country of the Arabs. He leveled the heads and diadems of many sovereigns and crown-bearers with the earth and

[19] Sultan Orḫan is left out of this enumeration, probably by mistake; he is counted below, when, e.g., Murād III is rightly called the 12th sultan.

[20] These are the pre-muslim names of resp. Mecca and Medina, cf. ʿAlī Cevād, *Memālik-i ʿOsmāniyyeniñ tāriḫ ve coġrafiyā luġati*, 4 Vols. (Istanbul 1313), I 179.

[21] I.e. Al-Ḥasā : a region on the Arab peninsula at the Persian Gulf south of Kuwayt.

[22] I.e. Bāyezīd I (1389-1402). He was defeated by the *ṣāḥib-ḳıran* Timur Leng in 1402 in the Battle of Ankara and led away as prisoner of war (and, in ʿĀlī's view, a victim of his own pointless resistance against a God-sent ruler).

[23] These are provinces in Anatolia. The province of Rūm must not be confused with Rūm in its general meaning which referred to the Ottoman Empire.

[24] I.e. Meḥmed II (1444-1446 and 1451-1481).

punished powerful but erring men like Uzun Ḥasan [25], ruler of Persia, and scattered especially the blood of army commanders over the black soil.

In the same way Sultan Selīm H̱ān [26], ninth in the dynastic line, conquered during
(5a:1) his reign Egypt, Syria and Aleppo, and was even able to mention the title of Servitor of the two sacred Fanes in his beautiful sermon. He tucked up [the sleeves of] his influence-increasing forearm, especially to defeat a *ṣāḥib-ḫurūc* like Shah Ismāʿīl of Ardabil [27], to revenge himself by killing a powerful man such as the sultan of Egypt, Ḳanṣu Ġavrī [28], and to bring order to all countries by his many brilliant conquests within only 8 years' time.

But Süleymān H̱ān [29] who was a country-conquering shahinshah of the tenth generation, reigned for 48 years with justice. He was a padishah worthy of Chosraw who was blessed with a long and glorious life of 74 years, and made many conquests and waged many holy wars. He made it evident that the boundaries of the well protected dominions had reached under his extremely auspicious reign their utmost limit with [provinces] such as Basra, Laḥsā, Abyssinia and Jemen, and occupied countries which contained, on the whole, 20 *beglerbegilik*s. He showed preference for the chiefs of the *ʿulemā*, protected the leading poets, exerted his utmost influence in favour of the 'men of the pen' (i.e. the officials and bureaucrats in his service) and gave his full attention to the 'men of the sword' (i.e. the military class).

On the other hand, during the reign of his son Selīm H̱ān [30], whose distinguished nature was free of defects, a noble man to whom respect was due, and who was so fortunate as to ascend on the throne, one had a good time of it, [much money] was spent, and the world-order, up to a certain point, began to to show [signs of] discomposure, because his Grand vizier Meḥmed Paşa [31], a man of exalted rank and a fine disposition who was his son-in-law and a pillar to the edifice of the dynasty of the cultivated lands, advanced his relatives and relations whenever he saw a chance to do so, thus promoting many parvenus and appointing them to lofty positions. Consequently, the ordered system of the affairs of mankind was changed in a way, and many of the great men as well as the common people gulped down bowl after bowl of poison at the banquet of his effrontery.

[25] I.e. Uzun Ḥasan (1453-1478) of the Aḳḳoyunlu dynasty. He was defeated by the Ottoman army in 1473 near Tercān.

[26] I.e. Selīm I (1512-1520).

[27] A *ṣāḥib-ḫurūc* was a great conqueror of, probably, also religiously obscure origin. Shah Ismāʿīl I (1501-1524) was defeated in 1514 near Çaldıran.

[28] The Mamlūk sultan Ḳansūḥ al-Ġawrī (1501-1516) as his name is also spelt in Arabic, was killed in 1516 in the Battle of Marj Dābiq near Aleppo.

[29] Sultan Süleymān *Ḳānūnī* ('The Law-giver') (1520-1566).

[30] Sultan Selīm II (1566-1574). He was born in 1494.

[31] I.e. Soḳollu Meḥmed Paşa (1505-1579), grand vizier 1565-1579.

(15) Although the sovereign of the world, the above-mentioned Selīm Ḫān, did not loosen the reins [of his authority] so much as to permit arrangements contrary to the 'old law' (*ḳānūn-i ḳadīm*) or follow, at every turn, the paths, suggested by him (i.e. Meḥmed Paşa), that were contrary to his grace, the fact, nevertheless, that a son-in-law of this kind, being traditionally favoured with the rank of grand vizier, is a prop to the dynasty of this country, and the fact, moreover, that this sovereign in the position of Jam[32] was, by day and night, being found fuddled and drunk by a feverish intoxication of wine, were reasons for the complete independence of the above-mentioned advisor, and especially for his unrivalled and exalted position in the valleys of commerce where he did as he liked and deemed proper. Whatever he (i.e. Meḥmed Paşa) proposed then, he (i.e. the sultan)
(20) would not oppose, but it sometimes happened that he (Meḥmed Paşa) did not even proceed to submit petitions (*'arż u 'alām*)[33] for offices in which he appointed his protégés. Thus, the state of health (*mizāc*) of the Empire was impaired by the unwholesome vice of the period: the acidity of inharmonious activities jaundiced its rosy face, and the mad desire to procure silver and gold, and the sick and melancholy love of the epoch for money and property, changed for the worse by the outbreak of bilious fevers.

A minute investigation

(5b:1) Learned men have agreed [on the fact that] the disruption of the workshop of the Empire, i.e. the Ottoman state, was caused by three [cases of] base ingratitude, each of which implicated a breach of faith[34].

The first case was the deceitful murder and elimination of the prince called Sultan Muṣṭafā, the most rightfully entitled heir to the sovereignty, by Rüstem Paşa[35], son-in-law of Sultan Süleymān. *The second case* concerned the selfish bargaining by which the above-mentioned Meḥmed Paşa, son-in-law of Sultan Selīm Ḫān, turned over high functions to his followers. *The third case* was the misleading and

[32] I.e. Jamshīd, one of the legendary Persian Kings of the *Šahnāma*.

[33] These official 'petitions' were called *'arż* and later more generally: *telḫīṣ*, see: Suraiya Faroqhi, *Die Vorlage (telhis) des Gross-wesirs Sinan Paša an Sultan Murad III* (Diss. Hamburg 1967), 18. The words *'arż u i'lām* (and perhaps the *'arż u 'alām*, of the same meaning, of our text is a mistake) were part of the fixed formula of these documents, see: L. Fekete, *Einführung in die osmanisch-türkische Diplomatik der türkischen Botmässigkeit in Ungarn* (Budapest 1926), lx.

[34] In the text: *raḫne*, lit. 'a breach in a wall'.

[35] Rüstem Paşa (d. 1561) was *dāmād* ('son-in-law') of Sultan Süleymān and grand vizier from 1555 to 1561. After the death of the sultan's mother in 1534 he became one of the most influential personalities at the Court in Istanbul. He got involved in a plot organized by the wife of the sultan, Ḫurrem Sultan (Roxelana), to eliminate the crown-prince Muṣṭafā who was a favorite of the *'ulemā* and threatened to become too powerful for the plotting court-faction. The murdering of the prince in 1553 shocked the country and caused the fall of the grand vizier.

perverting by which Şemsī Aḥmed Paşa[36] of the family of İsfendiyār, who had worked his way up from the *beglerbegilik* of Rumeli and favoured his good fortune by being a companion (*muṣāḥib*) of the sovereign, filled Sultan Murād Ḫān with a longing for bribes.

Without fail, these three [cases of] base ingratitude shook the four walls of the Empire with three single blows, and it is clear as daylight that the great quantity of bribes brought near the setting of the sun of its dynasty according to the saying: "How long will the sun of this epoch (i.e. the reigning sultan) remain the glory of the palace?". The rising and appearance of the signs of setting and descent moved the world-order to another phase and destroyed and annihilated this flourishing House down to its foundation.

[A poem] by the author

When the temper of the world was stricken with decease
    the ruler should have turned physician.
But the ruler too has fallen ill,
    he knows the symptoms of sickness have spread.
Gradually the disease became chronic;
    the longer it has lasted, the more severe its effects.
As long as the doctor does not prescribe the tonic of justice
    how can the forlorn patient be saved?
Cupidity is a special, horrid affliction;
    melancholia is difficult to cure[37].

Prose

As we have explained, the first symptoms of the beginning disruption had been established during the period of Sultan Selīm; the officials in high positions had become vagrants, their wanderings were unaccountable and they were inevitably recorded in a chapter of the book of bribery. The dwellers of the Most High Harem and all boon-companions did not really interfere with the affairs of state, and the secrets of state and dynasty did not come to light and were not discussed by the common people, so much so that a poet of the period, Mevlānā Fehmī[38]

[36] For him, see the *Introduction*, p. 10.

[37] I adopt here Fleischer's translation, '"Ibn Khaldûnism"', 213.

[38] He died in 1591. In his *Ḥālatu'l-Ḳāhire* ('The Conditions of Cairo') of 1599 (edited by A. Tietze, Vienna 1975), 'Ālī also quotes a poem of this man in which he criticizes Sinān Paşa, see: Tietze, *Muṣṭafā 'Ālī's Description of Cairo of 1599*, translation, 75-76. Mevlānā Fehmī was a son of the writer Ḳınalizāde 'Alī Çelebī whom 'Ālī had met in Damascus during the sixties.

recited this small poem (*ḳıṭʿa*) and presented it to the Illustrious Friend (i.e. the sultan) in the form of a petition (*ʿarż-i ḥāl*):

A small poem of Fehmī

Nobody ever informs you about the situation of the world,
    the sultan of the time has remained behind his screen,
His ministers are only anxious to collect money,
    while everybody is tormented by the fire of poverty.
Müftī nor *sheyḫ* tell this secret to the shah of the world.
    If one said: "Reveal it!", they say: "Don't worry!", but they don't commit it to paper.

(20) *The story*

The moral of the story which I explained in detail [above] is, this: the cause [of the fact] that the great fame of the outstanding among the preceding sultans and the virtuous of the noble emperors who came and disappeared [again], will remain alive until the day of resurrection and that the events of their proud reigns will endure and last on the pages of days and the leaves of months and years through the histories with their various stories, and the reason, moreover, why their noble souls are cheered with auspicious blessings when they are mentioned in one literary séance after another, are the books and works of the *ʿulemā*
(6a:1) from among the writers of their reigns, and the fragments (*muḳaṭṭaʿ*s), odes (*ḳaṣīde*s) and other righteous poetry written by the poets from among the silver-tongued eloquent. They recorded the stories of the leading personalities of the past, and took notice of, and showed inclination to the saying: "The most delightful thing to do, is to recite histories of the rulers". Therefore they have been honourable successors to the men preceding them and have been worthy of the prayer: "God has pardoned what is gone"[39].

(5) Of this praiseworthy group, it was ʿĀşıḳ Paşa, son of Muḫlıṣ Paşa[40] (he was joined with God, and a spiritual guide of godfearing and pious men, loved by *şeyḫ*s looking for the right guidance), the blessed spirit from among the historians Mevlānā Rūḥī of Edirne[41], the prolix Monlā Neşrī[42] (he thoroughly studied

[39] Koran, sura 5:96.

[40] ʿĀşıḳpaşazāde (d. between 1481 and 1503) participated as a dervish in several military expeditions against the infidels. He was one of the first important Ottoman historians who wrote in Turkish.

[41] Rūḥī (d. after 1511). Of his biography almost nothing is known. He perhaps had a position at the Court in Edirne. He wrote an Ottoman history in Turkish up to the year 1511. See: V. L. Ménage, 'Edirneli Ruhi'ye atfedilen Osmanlı tarihinden iki parça', in: *İsmail Hakki Uzunçarşılı'ya Armağan* (Ankara 1976), 313 and 328.

[42] His biography is very obscure, cf. V. L. Ménage, *Neşhrī's History of the Ottomans* (London 1964), 6-7.

stories and works) and the writer of the book called 'The Compendium of Hidden Things' Mevlānā ʿĪsā of Ḥamīd[43] of landable conduct, who, first of all, wrote histories of the House of ʿOs̱mān and recorded, according to the requirements of their time, stories and strange events that occurred until the age of Sultan Bāyezīd Ḫān and Sultan Meḥmed Ḫān[44] in poetry and prose.

Although it is known that they were not authors and writers in the acceptable, official style (*münşīs*), because of their writing and works the events of their days which they described are at least not forgotten or concealed.

[A poem] by the author

They brought to life the fame of kings,
    may God have mercy upon them all!

After them, the matchless historian, a writer versed in eloquence, envied by Ibnu'l-Aṯīr[45] and popularized through the words of Ibn Ğarīr[46], the famous *münşī* Monlā Īdrīs[47] who honoured the soil of Rum [by his presence] during the time of Sultan Meḥmed the Conqueror, wrote his 'Histories of the House of ʿOs̱mān' on his (i.e. the sultan's) agreeable order. This really is an eloquent book. It bears the title 'The Eight Paradises'[48], and has no faults apart from, herc and there, some entanglements and oddities, but there are much more ambiguities (*ibhāmāt*), metaphores (*kināyāt*), double-entendres (*tevriye*), homonymies (*tecnīsāt*) and stylistic devices (? *taʿbiye*) than were to be hoped for. It is as if the details of thc stories proper are more numerous than the samples of the [different] categories of letters [he used]. If he had come more within reach of the understanding of the people of Rum, it would have been impossible to find his equal, and it became clear that if he had sweetened his most strange words by [adding] world-conquering expressions, the content of his writings had not caused ennui. In consequence of its difficulty (i.e. of Bidlīsī's writing) Sultan Bāyezīd Ḫān, son of Meḥmed Ḫān[49], prompted by some courtiers, commissioned

43 Of this historiographer nothing is known, see *Introduction*, p. 8. Ḥamīd is the name of a province in southern Anatolia.

44 I.e. sultan Bāyezīd II (1481-1512), and Meḥmed II (1444-1481).

45 I.e. ʿIzzu'd-dīn Ibnu'l-Aṯīr (d. 1234). an Arab historian of fame. ʿĀlī mentions him in his enumeration of sources in the first *rükn*, *KA* I, 17:27 and 29.

46 I.e. the historian Muḥammad b. Ğarīr aṭ-Ṭabarī (d. 923), cf. *Introduction*, p. 5-6.

47 I.e. Īdrīs Bidlīsī (d. 1520). See for his biography and work in particular: V. L. Ménage, 'Bidlīsī', in *EI*² (*Encyclopedia of Islam*, 2nd ed.), 1207.

48 The 'Eight Paradises' corresponded to the reigns of the eight Ottoman sultans from ʿOs̱mān to Bāyezīd II.

49 I.e. Bāyezīd II.

at the same time a professor (*müderris*), Aḥmed, son of the deceased Kemāl Paşa[50], to write a book in Turkish, and, truely, he wrote well, and expressed himself in the clear and plain style used in that time.

When we come to the time of Sultan Süleymān Ḫān [we see that] it was *nişāncı*
(6b:1) (*mīr-i nişānī*) Celālzāde[51], whose fine name was Muṣṭafā, and namesake of the
Prince of Prophets, affixer of signatures (*müvaḳḳi'*) of the sultan's *Dīvān* and writer of the imperial cypher (*tuġrā-keş*), who wrote a widely diffused book with the title of 'The Classification of Countries'[52], and described in an orderly way the customs and manners of the House of 'Os̱mān.

(5) After a while there appeared a book, emanating from the pendrops of the affixer
of signatures (*müvaḳḳi'*) of the *Dīvān*, *Mīr* Meḥmed, son of Ramażān[53], who was, bearing the title of *nişānī*, a buttress among the pillars [of state], and famous for his office[54]. By writing his 'Histories of the Ottomans'[55], he felt he rendered a service due to the writers of the imperial cypher (*tuġrā-keşān*). Although he began his book with the creation, he wrote only a short [work] which he gave the form of a summary (*fihrist*) and did, in the end, not go beyond the size of a long essay.

Thereupon, it was Mevlānā Sa'du'd-dīn[56], son of Ḥasan Cān, an erudite person of a praiseworthy and quick understanding, a prop and stay of [the class] of professors (*müderrisīn*) and noteworthy for his studies, who wrote his 'Histories of the House of 'Os̱mān'[57]. He has a reputation adorned with eternity and is held in honour by people of distinction through his works. He really was superior
(10) to his predecessors who had written in Turkish and has won his spurs by his
achievement[58]. His choice of words is animating, his style natural and pleasant, and his stories are laudable. The way his introductions unfold is satisfactory and rewarding.

Thereupon, though, it became manifest and clear that the princes of the time were proceeding to collect money, that the illustrious viziers were eagerly devoting

[50] I.e. Kemāl Paşazāde (d. 1534). See esp. V. L. Ménage, 'Kemāl Pas̱ha-zāde', in : *EI*², IV, 879-881.

[51] I.e. Celālzāde Muṣṭafā Çelebi (d. 1567) also known as *Ḳoca Nişāncı*.

[52] This work has recently been edited by P. Kappert, Wiesbaden 1981.

[53] I.e. Ramażānzade Meḥmed Paşa (d. 1571) also known as *Küçük Nişāncı*. Both Celālzāde and Ramażānzāde 'Ālī had known personally during his studies in Istanbul, cf. Fleischer, 'Âlî', 50-51, and the *Introduction*, p. 10.

[54] Lit. 'pointed at with fingers (...)', see for this Arabic expression : H. Wehr, *Arabic-English Dictionary* (ed. by J. M. Cowan and transl. from the German, 3rd ed., New York 1976), 76.

[55] This work is more generally known as the *Tāriḫ-i Nişāncı* (Istanbul 1279).

[56] See for him : *Introduction*, p. 2 and 11.

[57] His work is more generally known as the *Tācu't-tevārīḫ* ('The Crown of Histories').

[58] Lit. : 'stamped his coining-die in marble', see for this expression : E. Kemal Eyüboğlu, *Onüçuncü yüzyıldan günümüze kadar Şiirde ve Halk Dilinde Atasözleri ve Deyimler*, II (Istanbul 1975), 323, no. 32.

themselves to the treasuring of gold and silver, that the leaders of the *ʿulemā* had retired in bewilderment with all their ambitions, that the leading scholars were sitting, one by one, depressed and silent in their corners, that advice and councel of preachers was [changing] according to the mood of the great men, and that the *şeyḫs* were carrying out [their functions as leaders of their] religious orders (*tarīḳat*) for a salary. While the accounts of great men and the common people were being settled because of their profane lies, and noble and virtuous men had to pay for their pious pretence (i.e. were being liquidated)[59], the scores of jesters were not demanded or even asked for.

[A poem] by the author

They felt disgust for knowledge and discourse,
 and descended into the niche of oblivion.
Know-nothings took the seats of the erudite,
 mighty men felt an inclination for ignorance.
The pearls and jewels they were wearing on their fingers,
 were cast behind their backs.
The great demeaned themselves, all of them,
 and fools, one by one, came out into the open.

When, thus, the circumstances of the time had become evident, criminals (lit. 'blacks') who had attained the level of literacy and claimed being guiltless, made their appearance as 'artists'. First of all, a person called Loḳmān[60], a cadi of ill-balanced words who was unwilling to take note of the words "Poetry calls for wisdom" and had no idea whatsoever what was meant by poetry and prose, suddenly became imperial *şehnāmegūy*, and one writer, a historian[61], even put
(7a:1) his signature under his chaotic poetry, saying: "Well done! [He, indeed, displays a] Lokman-like wisdom!"[62].

Thereupon a certain Nuṭḳī[63] (lit. 'the Talker'), a fool (lit. 'a speaking animal'), was deemed fit for the rank of *şehnāmegūy*. The position of Grand vizier of Poets was soiled by the appointment of an infamous person like him, a congenitally ignominious character, a fake rope-dancer, a so-called story-teller, and a boorish peasant who could be reckoned a Persian (*ʿAcem*) in all his clumsiness (*ʿacemīlik*).

59 Lit.: 'the register with figures on knowledge (...) was folded'.
60 See: *Introduction*, p. 11 ff.
61 This was Ḫōca Saʿduʾd-dīn, cf. *Introduction*, p. 11 and 13.
62 Lokman was the name of two legendary sages, of whom one was famous as a storyteller.
63 Cf. *Introduction*, p. 14 ff.

(5) Then, the rank of *şehnāmegūy* was, according to the saying "If a thing happens
twice, it happens three times", bestowed for the third time [by the appointment of]
the famous İbn-i Taʿlīḳī Meḥmed Çelebi[64] of praiseworthy behaviour, and this
noble and genial gentleman acquired world-wide fame by being so lucky as to
become *şehnāmegūy*. While all people, high and low, saw clearly that two of
these famous men, who were still flying as rooks and kites in the superior apsis
of the atmosphere of wild fancy, were greedy customers to buy a 'raven-letter'[65]
on the market-place injurious to mortal men, in order to show off their knowledge,
but obviously demonstrated no capacity and ability to understand the Story of
(10) the Ten Birds[66], and were, [on the whole], crack-brained and demented,
Taʿlīḳīzade, on the other hand, proceeding cautiously but elegantly, roused himself
to increasing splendour in his poetry and prose, and proved that in this atmosphere
of sin the pinions and wings of his talent were spread out.

[A poem] by the author

Although the universe-conquering Padishah did perhaps not
pay them the smallest attention from his elevated position,
He imagined that every one of them was well-versed in poetry,
and even proficient in writing a pure literary prose.
Therefore they profitted of the sultan's favour
(15) and obtained protection and gifts in abundance.
Two of them became honoured fief-holders (*zaʿīm*) of the time,
in the end, Nuṭḳī figured among them as the villain of the time.
The first two were given useful *zʿāmets*[67]
and their words were heard and esteemed.

Prose

To make a long story short: during the days that Sultan Selīm Ḫān[68], keeper of Jamshīd's glass[69], was fighting in the Council of State for the growth of the

[64] See: p. 13-14.

[65] This 'raven-letter' perhaps alludes to a scene in the Persian *Marzūbān-nāma* in which a raven tries to ingratiate himself with the King of the Lions with information about a threatening assault by the King of the Elephants, and begs for a 'letter of thanks', see the translation by R. Levy, *The Tale of Marzuban* (London 1959), 183-186, but perhaps it means more simply an anonymous letter of denunciation like the French *corbeau* (suggested to me by Ethel Portnoy).

[66] The 'Story of the Ten Birds' perhaps is the didactical *meṣnevī* of Şemsī of the same title, cf. E. J. W. Gibb, *A History of Ottoman Poetry*, 6 vols (London 1900-1909), II, 383-385.

[67] A *zeʿāmet* was a military fief with an annual return of twenty to hundred thousand *aḳçe*.

[68] I.e. Sultan Selīm II.

[69] The 'glass' or 'mirror' of Jam(shīd) symbolizes the world.

Empire, *re'īsü'l-küttāb* ('Chief of the clerks') *Mīr* Ferīdūn[70], son of ʿAbdu'l-Celīl,
(20) who, as a so-called all-round secretary, was closely involved in the private affairs of Grand vizier Meḥmed Paşa 'the Tall One'[71] and was a honoured man, whose qualities dayly increased, secured the protection of the above mentioned Loḳmān by his pasha. He (i.e. Soḳollu Meḥmed Paşa), on his turn, thought it proper that he (i.e. Loḳmān) became *şehnāmegūy*. Being a favourite cadi of a provincial town, he was instructed to versify for a most precious *zeʿāmet*. So he berhymed what he found during the reign of the generous Murād H̱ān[72], righteous son of the above
(7b:1) mentioned Sultan Selīm. How long did not the master of the eloquent, Firdawsī of Ṭūs[73], have to swallow in the spiritual world the poison of imitation and reproduction of the above-mentioned [Loḳmān]! While the spirit of this sage was afflicted by the misfortune of another torture, and his sorrow and grief increased thousand-fold because the above mentioned Persian (or: inexperienced, *ʿacemī*)
(5) Nuṭḳī had become *şehnāmegūy*, it was clear that he found some sort of confort when this imperial function fell vacant and Taʿlīḳīzāde was appointed, and that the triple rank of potential versifiers was not completely sunken and debased, the more so, because in his book it was explained that this scion of the Fenārī family, which is considered an illustrious race among the *ʿulemā*, was an intelligent gentleman and an unequalled outsider. In his preface to the 'History of the Ottoman Dynasty'[74], namely, he described his situation with the following verse:

His poetry

I said: "May God facilitate that I attain
   the positions of my father and grand-father,
May I, weak as I am, obtain a high rank,
   when young shah Murād comes to reign!
I have interpreted many books;
   may I continue to do so for many years more!"
(10) Thereupon, a great restoration took place:
   the imperial accession to the throne was excellent.
They appointed me *şehnāmegūy* to the shah,
   but wore my lamenting body to a hair.

[70] Ferīdūn Aḥmed Beg (d. 1583) was for a long time private-secretary to Soḳollu Meḥmed Paşa, and is famous for a collection of official letters which he edited.
[71] I.e. Soḳollu Meḥmed Paşa.
[72] I.e. Sultan Murād III.
[73] I.e. the writer of the *Šāhnāma* mentioned above.
[74] This probably is his *Şemāyilnāme* which is his only work that is close to a general history of the Ottoman dynasty, cf. Woodhead, *Şehnāme*, 9-13.

In any case, the [first] two versifiers of praiseworthy diction opened a market for the composing of a world of poetry, and did their utmost to [eulogize] the beautiful qualities of the great sultans who were the objects of their praise. Presently, some of the above-mentioned Monlā Loḳmān's couplets in Persian and a *ḳıṭ'a* of his in Turkish are reproduced to demonstrate, in their essence, his perfect eloquence and linguistic skill:

His poetry in Persian

In seventy-five of the eighth century[75],
a precious pearl fell into the jewelry-case of the shah;
A drop from the April-sea of knowledge
an animated source for a man of understanding.
From God's bounty he asked a crown for his head
and wisdom for his healthy (*selīm*) being.
His accession took place in ninehundred and eighteen[76],
the protection of God, always his Friend and Fellow-traveller, was with him.
Both Arab and Persian were subdued,
he knocked down the idols in the country of 'Os̱mān.

and his poetry in Turkish

Ta'līḳīzāde, that respectable gentleman, conceived a strange
idea. He thought: "If my *Şehnāme*
is in Turkish, it is the same story again:
the moment I speak, I will be overcome by Persian.
This is a heavy task. But what if I took for some feet
that beautiful language as a companion?"

Apart from these [lines], he said in his book, called *Şemāyilnāme*[77] in which he described Sultan Murād H̱ān, in order to encourage him to fight:

[75] I.e. 1470/71. The sources are contradictory on the matter of the date of birth of this sultan, Selim I. Cf. Ş. Altundağ, 'Selîm I', in: *İA* X, 423.
[76] I.e. 1512.
[77] For this work, see: *Introduction*, p. 13.

His poetry

It is time, o shah, let us prepare ourselves for combat!
Let us decide definitively to repulse the enemy!
Let us conquer Iran from end to end!
Let us have our share there as princes and pashas!
Let us defeat and scatter the tribes of Timur,
(8a:1) and let us leave a pleasant memorial to the world!
If Timur Leng destroyed the mosques,
let us build [them anew on] the places where he destroyed them!
If he took captives from among the Muslims,
let us free them, young and old!
He, whose dynasty is oppressive,
who is, like Timur, master everywhere,
Waxes out, like a young snake, into an imperial serpent,
with a cold face, filled with poison, and unclean.

The story

Taʿlīḳīzāde was a unique and eminent man, free of malevolent intent and afterthought, and the plate of his mind was untouched by the rust of attachments; he did not, like the others, talk incoherently, and his poetry and prose ware distinguishable from one another. His elegant rhymed prose, into which his significant thoughts were cast, was not only sound and full of contrast, but also its following and preceding context and tenor were conveniently arranged. He was a relater of anecdotes of the right moral quality, just because he was exceptionally elevated, even above the most exalted ranks occupied by the most supreme personalities. Thus, he composed the following distichs well: he had swallowed his faults and turned by now into the path of his great ancestors.

Nobody says that heaven is higher,
but perhaps he is wanting in discrimination[78].
Perhaps he is ignorant and foolish,
or mad and heedless like me
When he says: "I have read in a book
that the sun is brighter than the moon".

Thereupon he set out with Sultan Meḥmed H̱ān, son of Sultan Murād H̱ān, padishah of the world, and commander of great and small, to capture the fortress

[78] Lit.: 'he does not know to distinguish [it] from a rope', see for this expression: F. Steingass, *Persian-English Dictionary* (London 1892), 60.

of Egri[79]. It is deemed proper to recite now some of the matchless distichs which he has written after its capture and conquest as 'Turkish poetry', and it is ventured to copy here, be it obscurely and in rough draft, [these examples from] his imperishable stock [of poetry]:

In praise of the lords of his age, he said:

'How many firewood-splitting Turks with the temperament of an ass
    are worthy of the pack-saddle, or even the donkey-saddle[80]?'
He piles up his writings on the wall as if they are bricks,
    one on top of the other, this ill-natured man.
Reading them, you do not detect any meaning.
    If you inquire after their form, he loses his way amidst their verbs, particles and nouns.
If the discussion comes to medical treatment, he ascribes [his ailments] to grief.
    If you inquire after his blasphemy, he says it is inspired by his belief.
But while the truth is that his worthlessness is evident,
    and his fraud is clear, a thousand times over[81],
He always will find his place, this bastard,
    as the direct object is for ever put into the accusative.
He mounts on his fringed cloak of coarse, homespun cloth,
    so that the wind makes its tassels flutter.

To boast and to commemorate the shahs, [*saying*] "*I will animate them by my questioning*", [*the following lines*] *escaped him*[82]:

'I am an ocean of art, an overflowing sea,
    because I am like someone who empties a glass, gulp after gulp'.
He was incapable to eulogize the dynasty,
    the doubled feet worried him sick.
'I raise the value of the shahs,
    and praise those who wear the crown of Jam,
Exalting their courage, I am the ceroplast of shahs,
    the hoof of their noble steed which rubs the ground.

[79] See the *Introduction*, p. 3-4.
[80] See for 'donkey-saddle' (*ikāf*): *Vocabulaire Arabe-Français à l'usage des Étudiants* (anon. ed., Beyrut 1883), 8.
[81] Lit.: 'as if it be fourty'.
[82] I am not sure how to read this heading, and the translation consequently is uncertain.

A torrent of mortality took away the Seljuq dynasty[83],
and brought distress on the lineage of ʿAbbās the Grim[84].
Where are the great Būyids[85],
where the pure-minded Ṭāhirids[86]?
(margin) Where the dynasty of the iron-melting Ṣaffār?[87]
Where the proud Sarbedārids?[88]
Solomon, master of many servants
made them hostages of mortality, hostages of nonentity'.
We desire from the science of history
that Rustam and Kaiqubad become known[89],
(8b:1) But this work, the so-called 'Book of Kaiqubād'[90],
leaves, page after page, a rotten impression.
If one were to recite: 'This demon of steel,
lord of mace, battle-axe and scaling-ladder',
If one were to say: 'The demon Akvān[91],
spade of the execrable demons and great prince, digging for crimes',
He would perhaps see in his imagination quadrupeds in the Demavand Mountains,
or tents in the Caspian Desert,
and perhaps mistake Siyāvuš[92] for, a wild beast in the desert.
If he were to see me, he would even think I was Raḫš[93]!

Prose

(5) Although some verses in his book are better than the others, many of his products are similar to these. But if we take into account the waste of time [this implicated], we sufficiently flattered him and showed him enough courtesy by [quoting] this much [of his verse].

[83] The Seljūks reigned during the 11th-12th centuries over large parts of Iran and Syria; the Seljūks of Rum from 1077 till 1307 in Anatolia.
[84] I.e. the Prophet's uncle after whom the ʿAbbāsids were named and from whom they supposedly descended.
[85] The Būyids reigned over large parts of Iran in the 10th and 11th centuries.
[86] The Ṭāhirids ruled over Khorāsān during the 9th century.
[87] I.e. Yaʿqūb b. Layṯ as-Ṣaffār, lit. 'The Coppersmith'. The Ṣaffārids reigned over Sīstān from ca. 900 till ca 1495.
[88] The Sarbedārids ruled over Sabzavār in the 14th century; their nickname *sar-be-dār* lit. means 'with the head in a noose'.
[89] Rustam and Kaiqubād are both heroes from the *Šāhnāma*.
[90] With this work is perhaps meant his (Taʿlīḳīzāde's) *Şehnāme-i hümāyūn*, cf. Babinger, *GOW*, 167-168, and Woodhead, *Şehnāme*, 12 and 15ff.
[91] Akvān is a demon figuring in the *Šāhnāma* and destroyed by Rustam.
[92] Siyāvuš equally is one of the heroes of the *Šāhnāma*.
[93] Raḫš is the horse of Rustam.

There are, in particular, also his Persian poems. Most of them are acceptable, elegant and reverent. Although in each of them the instances of personal poetic licences (*taṣarrufāt*) are innumerable, they are all acceptable, deserving our sympathy and praiseworthy. But when Mevlānā Nuṭḳī had to stand the test and to exhibit the conch-shell of his words and their pearls strung in a precious fashion, he debased the traditional poetic art by reciting poetry of an unpredicted style. The truth is that he, unlike his debauchee but fully repenting predecessor, did not mend the flaws inherent of his poetry and prose.

The story

I saw that the conditions of the world were inverted everywhere and that the great men of our communities, the grand viziers, were red-hot and spellbound with love for the world. For more than 52 years of my life the cries: "[It is time] to leave, once more, to leave" reached, time and again, the channel of my ear, but as soon as the devine rains began to trickle, I opened my eyes from the slumbers of sleep to do Him honour. I consulted myself and scattered the pearls of these jewel-strewing distichs over my dust-like nature:

Poetry

Woe unto him who walks 50 years a-sleep,
    or did you suffer these 5 days
to make your prayer be heard?

Poetry

    to direct yourself towards two prayer-niches at the same time?

Without fail and seeking help from the Bestower of abundant wisdom, I began to write the 'Essence of Histories' in order to lay up a store of provisions for the hereafter, and thought it proper that the thirsty Muslims would benefit of its cool water of knowledge, until, at last, with the help of the Forgiving Creator, I concluded writing the four volumes, of which the fourth tells the stories of the history of the Ottoman dynasty.

I cherish the hope that God the Omnipotent—exalted be his power beyond disclosure and concealment—through his perfect wish and consideration, will turn around and circulate these four volumes throughout the seven climes of the inhabited quarter [of the world], and, in particular, will realize that the repute

of this illustrious copy will become generally known among the wise men of the times and will be an object of pride among accomplished clerks, in autumn and spring, day and night, like the 'Rose-garden' of Sheikh Sa'dī[94] and the 'Spring-garden' of Mawlānā Jāmī[95], and that, finally, the deceased forefathers, cloaked by God's pardon, the khans, served by servants and marked by knowledge, and the exalted Messenger of God the Omnipotent, who especially made unnumerable efforts [to produce] a fair copy from the rough drafts of this book, the fortunate commanding Brother whose abundant blessings are righteous and who is called
(9a:1) Muḥammad[96], will share in its success[97]. [I also hope] that it be realized and become true that the wishes of this writer, a sinner and criminal of regretful and perturbed thoughts, to partake of the happiness of this world and the next, will be gratified during his life, and that he will share in the privileges of praise in one literary séance after another, of uncomparable prayers and a rich reward.

God, the exalted Lord, knows and understands secrets, so that [he is aware] that I do not expect advantageous benefits from this writing, and do not hope for money of silver and gold because I realize and know that all work and effort, a desire for honour, decorum and dignity, and the display and monuments connected with the vicissitudes of this world are, like transitory life, a fleeting shadow.

[A poem] by the author

The purpose of this book is this:
  to banish distress and anxiety from my heart.
All I want is that God heeds me,
  that I will not incline and prostrate myself in worship for other men.
That he may provide me with a long life, and perfect knowledge and deeds,
  healthy descendants and a righteous existence,
truthfulness, and both repentance and an auspicious end,
  prolonged gratitude and a praiseworthy abode.
May God provide,
  that the sheets with my sins will be destroyed.

[94] Sa'dī (d. 1292) was an important Persian author. His *Gulistān* is a collection of didactic anecdotes in rhyming prose and verse.
[95] Jāmī (d. 1492), also a famous Persian writer. His *Bahāristān* is an elaborated imitation of the *Gulistān*.
[96] 'Ālī refers here, presumably, not (or not in the first place) to the Prophet himself—he would not be mentioned after the Ottoman 'forefathers' and sultans—but to his namesake Sultan Meḥmed III. I do not know what is meant by his 'efforts', but perhaps these should not be interpreted literally.
[97] Fleischer prefers here the reading (fol. 8b:23) *sa'ādet ve eẕiyyet-ile*, '(...) will share in its prospering and suffering'.

So that I do not need to fear for the Bridge and the Balance
and he will be contented with me, His slave.
So that I will not see the sparks of Hell's fire
and its smoke will not enter my eyes.
Let me witness my praiseworthy place in Paradise
in this present world.
Let my ideas not carry me too briskly away with them
for a swift profit on the market-place of public offices.
O my God, by the truth of every class of community,
o my God, by the truth of every living being,
that is, by the prayer of every nation,
(9a:13) make for me the favours of existence numberless!

SYNOPSIS OF THE CONTENTS OF THE PREFACE

(1) This chapter will give the reasons why the book, i.e. the fourth pillar of the *Künh*, is written. It intends to deal with the following points:
(a) the personal qualities and genealogical background of the Ottoman sultans;
(b) the historical facts of the establishment of the Ottoman dynasty between 700 and 1006 AH (1300-1597/98);
(c) the origins and political establishment of the dynasties in the countries surrounding the Ottoman Empire;
(d) the works written by some well-protected *'ulemā*; (3a:15-19)

(2) A writer (such as 'Ālī) who works hard and lets himself be guided by God's inspiration will, in the end, meet with success (ideally and materially), and will find recognition with (3a:20-3b:2)

(3) A poem by the author. (3b:2-5)

(4) The author wrote his book in the traditional way, recounting the stories, in particular those on the (Muslim) rulers and their customs, as they had been written by Ottoman historians and learned *'ulemā* until 1000 AH, (3b:6-11)

(There follows an ennumeration of the more or less contemporary Muslim rulers, and, mainly, some information about their position in the dynasty of which they were members:)

(5) Sultan Murād III (3b:11-14)
(6) Shah 'Abbās (3b:14-17)
(7) 'Abdullāh Ḫān (3b:17-21)
(8) Jalāluddin Akbar (3b:21-4a:1)
(9) Sherif Ḥasan b. Abī Numayy (4a:1-4)
(10) Ġāzī Gıray Ḥassān (4a:5-7)
(11) The last two mentioned rulers were subordinate to the Ottoman sultans.(4a:7-12)
(12) The shah of Persia and the Khaqan of the Turks (i.e. the Uzbekians), although they were not subordinate to the Ottoman sultans, showed them 'respect and love'. (4a:12-13)
(13) This was not the case with Jalāluddīn Akbar. The great distance of his country from Istanbul was considered an impediment to regular diplomatic relations. (4a:13-15)
(14) ('Ālī then enumerates the 'tribute-paying' infidel rulers and nations in Europe and the Caucasus who 'begged for submission' to the sultan) (4a:15-19)
(15) A poem by the author. (4a:20-4b:1)
(16) (There follows a summary of the Asian and north African countries subjugated by the Ottoman sultans from 'Os̱mān to Murād III, with the exception of Orḫan) (4b:1-13)
(17) The Empire under Murād III consisted of 40 *beglerbegiliks* that counted more than 300 *sancaḳbegis*, while on the other hand 'Os̱mān had ruled over only one *beglerbegilik*, that of Anatolia. (4b:13-17)
(18) Sultan Bāyezīd I who dared to resist the authority of Timur Leng, ruled only over Ḳaramān, Rūm and Rumeli. (4b:17-19)
(19) Sultan Meḥmed II, the conqueror of Constantinople, expanded his power ruthlessly over Anatolia and the Balkan up to Bosnia. (4b:19-23)
(20) Sultan Selīm I too, was able to expand the borders of the Empire, especially at the cost of Shah Ismā'īl and the Mamlūk Sultan Ḳanṣu Gavrī. (4b:23-5a:4)

(21) Under Sultan Süleymān the extension of the territory of the Empire reached its peak. He conquered another 20 *beglerbegiliks* and distinguished himself by his protection of the great *ʿulemā*, leading poets, civil servants and military men. (5a:4-9)
(There follows a long exposition on the decay of the Empire from the year 1553 onwards) (5a:9-5b:20)
(22) Under Sultan Selīm II 'the world-order began to show signs of discomposure': a pleasant life was pursued at Court and money was spent like water. This decay was caused by the treacherous activities of his grand-vizier Ṣoḳollu Meḥmed Paşa. (5a:9-14)
(23) The sultan, under pressure of the same Meḥmed Paşa, threatened to trespass the time-honoured rules of the *ḳānūn*: it was difficult to resist the suggested policies of the grand vizier who held a traditionally prestigious position, but also because he himself was continuously in his cups. (5a:14-20)
(24) The immorality and the lust for money of these times impaired the health of the Empire seriously. (5a:20-23)
(25) The decay was caused by three cases of base ingratitude:
(a) the murdering of Prince Muṣṭafā by Rüstem Paşa;
(b) the nepotism of Ṣoḳollu Meḥmed Paşa;
(c) the corrupting influence of Şemsī Aḥmed Paşa on Sultan Murād III. (5a:23-5b:6)
(26) These three facts shocked the state and dynasty to a degree that the fear of its collapse was actually justified. (5b:6-9)
(27) A poem by the author. (5b:10-12)
(28) The first effects of the decay were perceptable during the reign of Sultan Selīm II; but none of the courtiers raised his voice and the disorientated officials were inevitably corrupted by bribery. The general silence was broken by Mevlānā Fehmī. (5b:13-17)
(29) A critical *ḳıṭʿa* of Mevlānā Fehmī. (5b:18-19)
(30) The remembrance of the glorious deeds of the sultans persists through the prose and poetry of the eloquent *ʿulemā* and 'righteous men' which is recited in literary séances. (5b:20-6a:3)
(31) (ʿĀlī then comes to discuss the Ottoman historians of repute and some of their works:
(a) ʿĀşıḳ Paşa b. Muḫlıṣ Paşa;
(b) Mevlānā Rūḥī;
(c) Monlā Neşrī;
(d) Mevlānā ʿĪsā and his *Cāmiʿ üʾl-meknūnāt*;
(e) Monla Īdrīs and his *Heşt Bihişt*;
(f) Aḥmed b. Kemāl Paşa;
(g) *Mīr-i nişānī* Muṣṭafā Celālzāde and his *Ṭabaḳātu'l-memālik*;
(h) *Mīr* Meḥmed b. Ramażān and his *Tevārīḫ-i ʿOs̱māniyān*;
(i) Mevlānā Saʿduʾd-dīn b. Ḥasan Cān and his *Tevārīḫ-i āl-ʿOs̱mān*.
A couplet separates the earlier from the later historians in 6a:11) (6a:3-6b:11)
(32) In this time, alas, the 'princes and viziers' were in the grip of their lust for money, the great *ʿulemā* and learned men were retired and silenced and preachers and *şeyḫ*s were bribed by the leading personalities of the Empire. Essentially excellent men from all classes of society were liquidated on the flimsiest of accusations, while 'jesters' could do as they pleased without being called to account. (6b:11-17)
(33) A poem by the author. (6b:17-19)
(34) (Under these circumstances obscure preudo-literates had the chance to make promotion. Three of them were appointed as *şehnāmegūy* to the Court:
(a) Loḳmān;
(b) Nuṭḳī;
(c) İbn-i Taʿlīḳī Meḥmed Çelebi.

The first two had a very bad reputation, but the third proved to be able to turn his talents to profit. (6b:20-7a:12)
(35) A poem by the author. (7a:12-17)
(36) Lokmān was able to find favour at the Court and versify the events of the reign of Sultan Murād III, because he was patronized by Grand vizier Sokollu Meḥmed Paşa on the instigation of his private secretary *Mīr* Ferīdūn. (7a:17-7b:1)
(37) After the boorish Nuṭḳī, Ta'līḳīzāde was appointed. Being a member of the prestigious House of Fenārī, his reputation was better, and this in a way restored the soiled lustre of the *şehnāmegūylik*. (7b:1-7)
(38) A piece of his autobiographical poetry from the *Tārīḫ-i āl-i 'Osmānī* is now quoted. (7b:8-11)
(39) Even the first two mentioned poets in a way earn our esteem for the fact that they eulogized the sultans. (7b:11-11)
(40) ('Ālī then quotes verses of Lokmān: a Persian poem and a Turkish *ḳıṭ'a* which is directed against Ta'līḳīzāde) (7b:13-21)
(41) (There follows a quotation, a verse from the *Şemāyilnāme*, meant to exhort Sultan Murād III.) (7b:21-8a:3)
(42) Ta'līḳīzāde was in essence a capable man, and, now that he 'had swallowed his faults', well able to write poetry and prose of eminent quality. ('Ālī quotes one of his Persian poems) (8a:3-10)
(43) After the capture of Egri, at which he had been present, Ta'līḳīzāde wrote 'Turkish poetry'. ('Ālī quotes and satirizes some fragments from it) (8a:11-8b:4)
(44) Ta'līḳīzāde's Turkish poetry, indeed, was of an uneven quality, but his Persian verse was better. (8b:4-7)
(45) Unlike Lokmān, Mevlānā Nuṭḳī was altogether unable to avoid mistakes and proved incapable to compose verse true to the traditional canon. (8b:8-11)
(46) After more than 52 years of aimless wandering through a perverted world, 'Ālī was awakened by the 'trickle' of divine inspiration. (8b:10-14)
(47) Two fragments of his Persian poetry. (8b:14-15)
(48) 'Ālī began to write the *Künhü'l-aḫbār* and with God's help he was able to bring the four volumes to a conclusion as a benefit for the knowledge of the Muslims. (8b:15-18)
(49) 'Ālī cherished the hope that God would make his work famous in the world, that the 'forefathers', the sultans and especially sultan Meḥmed III would share in its success and that he might profit from its fame, although he knew that worldly renown was no more than a 'fleeting shadow'. (8b:18-9a:6)
(50) A poem by the author. (9a:6-13)

FACSIMILE OF THE LEIDEN PREFACE

3

سلطنت برله قلسون انتظام • روح اجداد اوبن الهبوب احیا • طورابادن اتسونلر ابا •

عدله میل السون وجودلری • کامل اولسون انسجا وجودلری • بخه سی اولدی خادم الحرمین •

قلدیلر کاتبانی لطفله زین • ایلدی دل خرابه سن معمور • بیت معموره بگزیه پر نور •

شهریار جهان اولان سلطان • که اوله برهمنام فخر عالمیان • ماله مایل کل حمد الله •

اولمسون کار و بار جاهی تباه • ارتشا در خراب ایدن دهری • لذت شهدی تلخ ایدن زهری •

نقد رشوت که ایده خزینه یی بر • کوزلر بیله سنی کوزتمی در • شهلک وارلغی رعایادر •

انلر اولمق خزینه اولی در • شنلسون اول خزینه بنی آدم • که اوله بر او طولوسی سیم و درم •

دم اولور سیم و زر بتور مزایش • خصم اولور صاحبینه نقد و کمش • ملکه قصد ایسه بر عدوی قوی •

مایمنه بردباری جند غوی • لازم اوله مدد اهل سیف و قلم • و بیره نا کم بنجه نوع و علم •

مالی انسان بعیز زواده الجون • جان و دل فوتن افاده الجون • بو قسیه بنزر نیم نکم زر و سیم

تیغه رابلن عدوتی دو بنم نشر و بالجمله پادشاهلرک خزینه سی رعیتلردر رعایانک لازمه سی

رعایت و ظلمه ظلمندن کندولرن صیانتدر • خزینه دکی نقود • حرق و غرقله نابود • وجنود

اولمه وعین مانده بی سود • اولمه سی قطعلندر • ما مار رعایانک هر بری بر کنز موجود • و کنج بر نقود •

درکه نار سوزان • وسیل فراوان • ایله ازاله سی • واضاعه سی نیز مستبعد دکی ما و لدر •

در سبب تألیف کتاب • و باعث تصنیف مستطاب • که آل عثمان اولان ملوک جهانبانک

حسب نسب ممدوح الخصالری • و سنه سیما بجری اولندن • سنه ثمن الف تاریخنه دک

ظهوره کلان سلاله و جهادانبا آثاری • و کندولرده ما صراولان ملوک اطرافک من جهة النسل

ظهور دنیاتلری • و کرسی مملکتلرنده کی تمکن و حکومت سماتری • مقدما حسن تربیتلرنه قابل

اولان بعض علما اعیانلرنک مجلا آثار و تالیفاترینی • بیابنده و ادلی جواد ذکر ادای موجزلرایله

شناح در یای زخار مداد که • عواطف عمان الهام و امداد • اولوب صدف مجره دوندن

وار دات جواهر بن بحار وتب • بارار رواج و اعتبار • و بهکذا نقادان و صیرفیان

ذوی الانظارده عرض نقد ایده کلمشلدر • و سیاح مدن و امصار سواد که بوادی کرد

رشد وسداد • و نواحی نور و فکرت فؤاد اولوب • ماورادی بحر محیط ظلمات و غیر

زترف بسیط و مرکب ایدن • قطرات آب حیات نوادرین حاصل قلوب هنروران دار اودبار
وخردپرور آن اعصار در روزگاره • عرض عقد گوهر عقد ایده گلمشدر لطیفه سی عبارات ایله دوتیدی آل عبا
بیاضه جعدی اوکنده سواد مرحامه • دلنده طی لسان طیلسانی نابشده عیان • مدام النده عصا فیلسوف علامه
کرکوکلده وددلنده عبارت اولمشدر • ایکی دلندن ایرر نظم ونثر انجام • پیر اولسه عنبر حمایله مجموعه سی
معطر اولمغه بشلر دباغ هنگامه • گرگ حامه در اول نخل میوه دار صفت • یابنده مردم ناچیده نکته دون نرحامه
باعث تسطیر اولان فحوای غرابی بویوردن املا قلدی • و سبب حادث تحریر صنوف عدد اولونان
مضمون دلگشای بو طرز ایله انشا ایلدیکه • تاریخ تصنیف وتالیف • که حساب مستطاب هجری ده
تمام الف الیف • وحوادث علوی و سفلی معلوم هر وضیع وشریف که • اولمشدی سلاطین
ممالک روی زمین • وخواقین ممالک معمورهٔ ارضین • یعنی اصحاب خطبه وسکه نامنده که شهریاران
ماندنشین • از مرز بوم روم بیرتمکین • تا سرحد هند وخطا وچین • کملر اندکه دونمو آئین
ودین • وترتیب وآئین • واحکام وقوانینله مشهور ایدوکلری شیوع کلی بولمشدی • بومنوال تحت
مال اوزره که دار الملک قسطنطنیه ده تخت نشین اولان زبدهٔ عثمانیان صاحب تاج ونگین
سلطان مرادخان ابن سلطان سلیم خان مغفرت قرین ایدی • که اوج یوز بیلدن بر وحد ایکان جهان
اولان تاجداران قوی تمکین سلسلهٔ علیه لرندن اون ایکی شهریار کامنیت وکامیاب • ایدی
ننه که ساکن پای تخت قزوین وممالک عجم سوادنده کی شهریار صدرنشین شاه عباس
ابن خدابنده بن شاه طهماسب رحلت گزین • اولوب شاهان اردبیلی سلالهٔ اسامیه سندن
یوز بیله قریب حکومت ایدنلرک یدنجی سپهر خسرو مسندنشین • ایدی بعده ماوراالنهرک
فرمان رانی وسمرقند کرسی سنک صدرنشین صاحب نشانی ملوک اوزبکیه دن عبدالله
خان بن اسکندر خان اولوب یوز اللی بیلدن برو اجرای احکام ایدن صاحب ظهور •
ابو الخیر داد علی دمحکله مشهور • ملک بزرگوار اولادنک اون ایکنجی سی بر کارفرمای مشترع •
وقوی دین ایدی • اما ملوک هندک جملهدن اشهری • خصوصا تیمور صاحب ظهور سلطانک
بشنجی شهریار تیموری سلطان جلال الدین بن سلطان همایون اولوب نسلی ایکی یوز بیلدن برو
رایان هندمیاننده اکبر ومظفر • ده کمال جود وسخا ایله • وبذل وبخشش عطا براجمله دن

مشهور

مشهورتر • بر پادشاه جلالت دستگاه بر ترین ایدیلر • بونلردن ماعدا اشرف بلاد امین و حاکم مکه

مکرمه گزین • صحیح النسب نامدار • وصریح الطلب بلند اشتهار • رأس الفقه وکف دورت نوربیلدن شرو بطنی

بر وار • و خطبه وسکه سی شهر وار و دیار • شریف حسن بن ابونمی اولوب الطه و یس

وسلاله سامیه خیر المرسلیندن کرمی بینسنده رتبه ده کی مسندنشین مکارم تمکین ایدی

لا سیما پای تخت ز حانی بقیه آل چنگز دولتمند ذی شان غازی کرای خان بن

دولت کرای خان اولوب اول نسل بزرکواردن اولان حکام تتار و ملوک عالی تبار کرامنده

برمی التنجی خان کار فرما و قوی تمکین ایدی • اکرچه که بو ذکر اولونان خان ذی شان • و شریف مکه

مکرمه نامنده کی صاحب قدر و عنوان • سکه و خطبه ایله مشهور عالمیان ایکی شهریار نامدار

ممالک ستاندر لکن سلاطین آل عثمانه عرض عبودیت ایدوب و قوات خطبه رفیعة الرتبه ده •

کندولر ملوک عثمانیه دن صکره ذکر اولنوب تحقیقلرین جکمکه معتاد • و اوامر عالیه لرینه مطیع

و منقاد و سر بر نشین اولمه ده دخی اکر اذن شریفلرینه کردن نهاده ایکی تاجدار لازم الاعتبار قوی

نژاد ایدوکلری عیاندر • مع ذلک شاه ملک عجم • و خاقان ترک معالی همم • کاه و بیکاه دعانامه لر

کوندررک • و عرض خلوص و تحبیه متابعت کوسترکمه آینه ظاهر و نمایاندر • انجق بو شرفدن

حرمان • جلال الدین اکبر خصوصنده واقع • زیرا که امد شد ایلچیانه بعد مسافه مانع عذاولندیغی

عرض اعتذارینه بر مانع دکلدر • ماریح مرقوم دکه سلاطین اهل اسلام • انجق بو ذکر اولونان •

خواقین عظام لازم الاعظام • و خراج کذاران عتبه علیالری نامنده کی رؤسای کفار ناقر جام

بنی کم اشبنیول • و پلجقو • ریم پاپ • ولونران • و عنده کرجستان و چرکس و دادیان •

واردل • و املاق • و روس • و بغدان • ولهو وچه وچار • و اکرو سرو الامان شاه ماه اله اکتنده

حنیان و غلطان • و اعلان عبودیت و ادبرینده • دامن در میان ایدوکلری معلوم اما ابا مدد

منتیه شهریاران ال عثمان • کردکار اندی خادم الحرمین • مملکت شرق و غرب آستانه لر

ضبط ایدرلردی مجدد ذو القرنین • مقلسلر سر کشانی دعوت اکر • کم علی الرأس العموم و کم علی العین

ابتیع او رتبه لقده جاریدر • اوله مرزانلو کله کسه هاین • پایمال اولمز بیولکر بینه •

مردی شام شانه یوز طوترشان • ترک جان فرض عین اولور مثلا • ساعدین و اجب الاداایدین

اورالمرد دن ۹۹۰ ع جوکنه سکر بوز ... ور ... وق سلیمان خلف اولان محمود اجمی ... وار بوسکری الجوجهاد ... و محمود ... دخل ... دن ... ان منکی صاحب ...

اوقونه سر ... ر عوز ... دار ... غالک ... سدن ... ان ابر ... ی ... مجھول طبقطه عشند ...

حاکم درکاهنه بوزسور نذر اولان • اجمل الجبهه اکحل العینین • القصه ممدوح • روشناسان دولت
ملوک آل عثمان که عثمان داد و اورخان و مراد خان و ییلدرم بایزید خان و سلطان محمد خان و سلطان
مراد خان و ابو الفتح سلطان محمد خان • خصوصا ابو الکرام سلطان بایزید خان و مصر قاهره فاتحی
سلطان سلیم خان و ولد سعید رشیدی • سلطان سلیمان خان و سه الدوله فرزند عزتمندی
سلیم خان و خلف صدق شرفی سلطان مراد خان • که زمان سلطنتلرنده تمامی ملک
روم و آبردی مرز و بوم اولان بلدان فسیحة الارجا • و اکثر سواد دیار عربک کافه مصر و شام
و حلب • کبیع لا بابات ابا کتنما • علی الخصوص حرمین شریفین • و نواحی یثرب و بطحا و اقالیم یمن
و عدن و حبشه و بصره و لحسا • لاسیما بزینه اکراد و موصل و دیاربکر و عراق عرب و آذربایجان
و ملک شروان • و کافه مدن و امصار کرجستان و وادیان داغستان مع ذلک جزایر غرب
و حلق الواد و تونس • و طرابلوس غرب و جزایر نیز بسر و رودس • آبا لسلری من الابتدا
الی الانتها • و عامه مضافات و ملحقاتنک حکومتلری • من القاصی الی الدانی • الحصول
بو سلسله جلیلهنک سلاسل فسخ و تسخیره چکلمش مضبوطلری • و قوة قاهره ایله مراو نوانینک
سلک ضبط و نفرلرینه منسلک محکوم و مربوطلری • اولمشدر مع ذلک تاریخ الفده واقع
اولان اکنجی بطنلری رابع سلطان مراد ثالث عنوانی ایله بخت نوزراوز زعاملکری لامع شهریار جهان پناه
بر پادشاه عالیجاه و مظفر سپاه ور که تلمرو حکومتی قرق مقداری بکلربکیلک تامل و افزون
زیاده بکلربکیلک مشتمل در حالا که حبه بز بر کو آ [illegible] تجرد تاطولی بکلربکیلکی عدد
اولوبان و لایته زمان [illegible] ایدی [illegible] دوردنجی قرنده واقع تیمور حادثه ظهور رفتنه سی ایله
شایع اولدر روم بایزید خان عصرینه کلنجه تلمرو حکومتلری الحق قرمان و روم و روم ایلی جمعا بکلربکیلک ایله موسوم
اولان مملکتلری که ظاهر و عیان ایدی اما بدنجی نسل شریفلری که ابو الفتح کشورستان قسطنطنیه
فاتحی سلطان محمد خان روم ایلی ولایتنی بوسنه سنورینه دک و اناطولی مملکتنی توسیع و تسخیر ایدوب
دیار عرب سرحدینه دک ایجدی [illegible] حاکم و تاجدار کسر و افریقیه حاکم یکسان [illegible] دیار
عجم شهریاری • اوزون حسن کبی قوی و غوینک حقندن کلوب خصوصا امرای عسکرینک فانی خاک
[illegible] ساجدی ننه کر فرزند سعادتمندی سلطان سلیم خان زمانده دولتنده مصر و شام و حلب تسخیر

نجز

5

تسخیر ایلدی حتی خادم الحرمین الشریفین الغایبی خطبه‌ی لطیفه‌سنده تذکیر ایدیلدی • لا سیما شاه اسمعیل
اردبیلی کبی صاحب خروجک انهزامنده • و مصر سلطانی قانصو غوری کبی بلند آوازک قتل و ... و
انتقامنده مجرد عسکر نیله بو مقدار فتوحات جلیله ایله عامه ممالکک انتظامنه شاهد مساعد
همتی تشمیر ایدیلدی • اما سلیمان خان که قرن عاشرده کی شاهنشاه ممالک ستاندر عدالتله
فرق عسکر نیل سلطنت ایلدی • بر پادشاه کسری سیر و تمش دورنده مقدار آن عمر عزیزلرنه
معمر اولوب نیچه فتح و نیچه غزا ایلدی • عهد همایون السعدنده کی ممالک محروسه سنورلری تا بمن و حسابه
و حبشه و یمن کبی سرحد منتهایه • منتهی ابدوکنی هویدا ایلدی • و بالجمله بکربکیلر بکلر ملکلرنه منسوب لی
اولوب صنادید علما به غبطت • و اجاو بد شوالنه رعایت • و ارباب قلمه جل همت • و اصحاب سیف
خرقه کلی التفات عنایت قلدی • که کلک فرزندی سلیم الطبع لمعار و خلف صاحب الشرف
لازم الاعزازلری سلیم خان که جلوس تخت سلطنتله کامران اولدی • زمان دولتلری عشق معروف
اولوب کندولرده آماده • و خاندان ملک معمورسنه عماد • اولان وکیل اعظم جلیل القدر نیکو نهاد
لری ... هنگام قرصنده اوبار تعلقاتندن ایلرو جمیکله • و نیچه نوکیسه‌لری قطع پایه ایله مراتب
سامیه‌یه نصب ایمکله نظام عالم بر مقدار اختلال ایله بوزلمدی • و انتظام احوال بنی آدم نوعا تبدل
اولوب نیچه اکابر و اعیانی ... نواله‌سندن کاسه کاسه زهر ایچوردی • اگرچه که شهریار جهان
مومی الیه سلیم خان قانون قدیمه مخالف اوضاعه ارخاء عنان ایتمزدی • حتی آنک دلالتی ایله
گاه و بیگاه خلاف همت اولان مذاهبه ... لکن اول مقوله وادیلره اعتقاد و قرار ...
کبریا پایه‌سی ایله خاندان ملکه عماد • اولمسی و سجدگاه ... اول شهریار جم ...
مداومت ... مشار الیهک ... استقلالنه • لا سیما دار ایستاده ...
علی قاپو ... جاه و جلالته • سبب اولوب هر نه عرض ایلسه مخالفت ایلمزدی • و بعض
محل اولوردی که توجیه ایلدوکی مناصبی عرض و علاوه و حق مباشرت ایتزدی بناء علیه ... راجح
عالم ملک اول دورده کی ذم فاسدله ... اولدی • و خصوصات اوضاع ناهموار • روی
گلگونی زرد ... و زمانه‌نک ... و منالله ... طولیاسی
صفراوی ... ایله ... تحقیق وقوع اتفاق عقلا ایله دولت عثمانیه‌نک ...

احتلال لنه اوج کفران النعمه‌نك بر رونقه القا ورخنه‌سی سبب اولمشدر که اوکی رحمه سلطان

سلیمانه دادا اولان رستم پاشانك کری ابله وآرشلحق ملکه اولان سلطان مصطفی پادشاهزاده

نك قتلنه وانلرك سببیله اکی حسنه وا ها مسلم جان اولان سابق الذکر محمد پاشانك ذوالفقاره

مذهب حالیه توجیه اولندوکی داد استاداننفسیدر اوج نجی رخنه ده امراء بکلکلرندن مقاعد

ومناصب شهریاری نامنه بخشی مساعد آل اسفندیاردن شمسی احمد پاشا سلطان مراد خانه

ترغیب ارتشا ابتدوکی اضلال واغواسیدر فلاجرم براوج رخنه چار دیوار ملکه اوج دولت

منزلزل قلدی وکثرت ارتشا شر العصر کم یقبل علی شرف القدر قوانینجه زوال بنیاد دولته

قریب العهد اولدوغی کون کبی روشن اولوب امارات افول وعزوبک طلوع وظهوری نظام

عالمی شکل آخره تحویل الدی واول ابنیه معموری استانه دک منهدم ومختل قلدی منشیه

عالمک چون مزاجی اولدی سقیم واجب اولدی که حاکم اوله حکیم بیک حاکم دخی اولونسه مرض

مرضنك مرض اكلادی نعره ... اولدی کسند نجه اول مرض ممتد نجه ممتد زیاده کشتند

شربت عدل الجوز بنجه طبیب نجه قورتلسون اول سقیم غریب جمع مال اوزره یخ مالدر

مالوبا علاجی مشکلدر نیشتر اکرچه که بیان اولندوغی اوزره اناد اوایل اختلال سلطان

سلیم زماننده ظهور ایدی اما ارباب مناصبک دریدر اولوب کرمه لر تکرر ابدی بنحالله

کتاب ارتشا بربابه درج اولونمشدر سکان حرم اعلی وسایر بنه‌ها حتی امور ملکه قارشدی

واسرار سلطنت وملک ابرودن طشره چقوب افواه عوامه دوشدی حتی اول عصرك

شعراسندن مولانا فهمی بو قطعه‌یی دیمشیدی عرضحال صوردنده پادشاه بزرگوار اره صوشدی

قصه‌سی فهمی برلیدر هرکسه بوغ احوال حالی سلطان دم قالدی ورادی جابه‌ده سر حلقه جمع قلندر

اما که نار فغزلرمرکس عزابده مفتی وشیخ زاده دبر شاه عالمه ایدر دیلسه دبرونی یازمز کتابده

القصه تفصیل قصه‌دن حصه بوردرکه کبار سلاطین سلف واحبار خواقین صاحب شرف

نك کوکب بخشلردر روز حشره دک نام بلندلری زنده وتواریخ مختلفه الزوال ابنالاه سرانجام

سلطنت منزلری صحایف ایام وصفایح شهور واعوامده باقی وپاینده اولنغه باعث

ومجالس محلس تذکر اولندیجه دعای خیرله روح شریفلری شاد قلنمغه بواعث زوال دو

دردی

رنده کی علمای مؤلفینک تصنیفات و آثاری • و نوادر بلغاء بلاغت گزینک مقطعات
و قصایدلر نظم ایدرلر کیمی • حکایات اعیان سلفی یازمشلردر الی الانبیاء تا آدمه
اخبار الحکمای مضمونینه التفات و رغبت گوسترمشلردر • اول جمله‌دن کندولر دخی سلطنه
صاحب شرف اولوب عفی الله عما سلف دعاسنه لیاقت حاصل ایتمشلردر • و اول زمره حمیده دن
اصحاب ورع و تقوی • محبوب مشایخ ذوی الاکرام‌دندر • و اصل جوهر عاشق پاشا بن مخلص پاشا
و زمره نورجینک روح بوالفتوحی ادرنوی مولانا روحی و منتبع قصص و آثار انشری
منتشر تعمار • و کتاب جامع الکنوز مؤلفی مولانا عیسی نام حمیدی حمیده کردار • که اولا تواریخ
آل عثمان تحریر ایتمشلر • سلطان بایزید خان بن سلطان محمد خان عصرینده دلتطویر •
ابد ذحوادث دهر ابی نظم و نثرله اقتضای زمانه کوره تسطیر ایتمشلر • اکثر احکامینی نوتوف
و منشی دکل ایدوکلری معلوم و ظاهر • و قلری حوادث ایامی الکوک معرر و آثاری ایمانسی •
و غیر منظوم • و درنشیه نظر تام ملوکی احیا • رحمة الله علیهم جمعا • بعده مورخ بی نظیر •
مؤلف بلاغت سمیر حسد کرده ابن اثیر • رواج برده تفتار ابن جریر • منشی
منشا ابد رئیس شیخیر کرابو الفتح سلطان محمد زماننده حاکی وقتی تشریف ایلدی • الرد
فرمان لطیفلری ایله تواریخ آل عثمانی تالیف ایلدی • حقا هشت بهشت نام بر کتاب
فصاحت فرجام • در که جابجا تعقید وعز ایتندن عبرد عیبی یوقدر • ابهام و کنایات
و توزیر و تجنیسات و تعبیره‌سی مأمول اولان مرتبه‌لردن چوقدر • تفاصیل حکایاتی خود نوبا
نما تبل صنوف حروفندن آرتوقدر • اگر اهل روم فهمنه اقرب اولسه • نظیر محال اولوردی
اغرب کلمات عالمگیرادی اراله اعذب اولسه • قال املاسی مؤرث ملال اولمدوسه •
تعیین بولوردی • حتی مسعودینه تبار کجعفر موالی ایالی سلطان بایزید خان بن محمد خان حضر •
الفا ایندیلر • اول زمانده زمره مدرسینده اولان احمد بن کمال پاشا مرحوم لسان
ترکی ایله تصنیف ایدر دیلر • الحق خوب یازمشلر اول زمانده مستعمل اولان بیان و اصطلاحه
بیان ایتمشلر • و فتی سلطان سلیمان زمانی اولدی • موقع دیوان سلطان
طغراکش ارکان خاقانی • جلال‌زاده بیر نشانی که نام لطیف مصطفی • و ممنام سلطان

انبا در طبقات الممالک نام بر کتاب منثور تألیف ایلدی • رسم و آیین آل عثمانی
علی الترتیب تصنیف ایلدی • بعده مدة موقع دیوان و نشانجی عنوانی ایله عمدهٔ
ارکان اولان میر محمد بن رمضان که انک منصبی ایله مشار الیه بالبنان اولدی
تألیف تواریخ عثمانیان خدمت لازمهٔ طغراکشان • اولمغین تصویری ایله بر
کتاب دخی انک رشحات اقلامندن ظهور و صدور بولدی • اگرچه که اول آفرینشدن
یازلمشدر • اما فهرست صورتی ایله اجمال تحریر ایدوب • بر رسالهٔ کبیره حجمنده اتمامه مشهور
بعد از آن عالم نادره دان فاضل ستوده اذعان • عمدهٔ مدرسین دار السلطنه
مولانا سعد الدین بن حسن جان بر سر مسند آرسته ذی شان • و تحریرات ایله انگشت
نمای اعیان • ایکن تواریخ آل عثمان یازدیلر • حقا که لسان ترکیده تألیف الهین اسلافه
تفوق ایدوب سکندر مرده فاخر دیلر • هم اداسی روح افزا و انشاسی مطبوع دلکشادر
هم حکایاتی دلارا و بسط مقدماتی مقبول و بنجادر • غب ذلک امرا و وزرا جمع
حاله سالک و وزرای بزرگوار ادخار زر و سیمه منهمک • مناصب علما حال جمیل گوشهٔ
انزواده مبهوت احاد و فضلا بر بوجه ده محزون او صاحب سکوت و انطلاک
بند و نصیحتی • اکابرک طبیعتلرینه کوره لازم • منباعک تکمیل طریقی بر امر معاش ایدوکی
روشن و واضح • اولوب کبار و صغار • مزخرفات دنیویه اعتبار ایتدی • اشراف و اخیار
حسنات دینیه اعتبار ایتدی • ارقام معارفک دفتری دورلدی • اصحاب لطایفک حسابی
نه طلب قلندی نه صور لدی • نتیجه بر تورلو افتی علم و هنرک • ایدیلر طایفهٔ نسیانه
فضلا سدر ریته کیدی جهلا • رغبت ایتدی اولولرنا دانه • الترا و زر ه قوتلو در زوجه
ردّ البیلد المطلوب یا بابه • ذلنده کتب نا کاتب حمله • چقدی بر بر سفها بید انه
چونکه احوال روزکار • بو منوال ایله آشکار • اولدی سواد خوان مرتبه سند هجی
روسیهلر یوز آقلوغی دعواسی ایله شعر و زرنامه وجود بلدی • دولا لقمان نام ان مس
الشعر طلکه مضمون نهنده ناکام • نظم و نثرک کمالی ادعا ایتدی نقصانی نام زمرهٔ
فضلادن بر شخص نامور دون کلام • بغتةً شهنامه گوی خاقانی اولدی • حتی ابو لعیس

مورخیندن

طرسی • عالم روحانیده نحر روزکار • مرنور کسر زهراب تقلید وتتبعی منضم ایلدی حالا کر
روح حکیم بر عذاب الیم بلاسنه دخی کرفتار اولدیا • یعنی کمذکور نطق عجمینک شهنامه کوی اولمسی الی
حزن دانه وهی بوایکن هزار • وقتی کم اول حدمت خاص کیدرک تعلیقی زاده یه دخی احضار
بولدی • نظم کلامه قادر اولانلرک اوج رتبه لری • بالکلیه تحضیض وتبت اولیوب بوغا
تسلیت بولمه لری تعیین بولدی • زیرا که بین العلما دوده مان بزرکوار اکملان آل
عثمانی بعتبه سی برخدمت عاقل ویکانه کی مماثل • ایدوکی کتابنده بیان اولنمشدر یعنی کم
منظومه تاریخ آل عثمانی دیباجه سنده بو ابیاتله وصف حالنی ابداع ایتمشدر نظم
ایام ودم منزلنه وصول • میسر اوله دیو نایکه حصول • وارورشه مرادجوان دولته
ارم دیبوبن ناتوان دولته • کتبدن نجه ترجمه ایلدوم • نجرس دخی کندوزم سویلدم
بوحال اوزره دورانی بلنس • جلوس همایون اولوب ارجمند • بنی شاه شهنامه کوی ایتدیلر
نتم مویه دن لیک موی ایتدیلر • علی کلی حال • بو ایکی نظم کوی ممدوح المقال • عالم نظمک
نظامنه رواج ویردیلر مدوحلری اولان • سلاطین عظامک اوصاف حسنه سنه کوشش قلدیلر
پس مزبور منلا لفانک زبان فارسیده واقع اولان ابیاتندن برفاج بیت دلستان
نرکیده کی نظمنده تعلیقی زاده یه معارضه بوزبیدن سویلدوکی قطعه • بو جلده ایراد اولنمشدر
که کمال بلاغتی و ذاللسانی اولدوغی قدرنی بونلردن کنهی اهل معلوم در نظمه فی لسان الدری
بهفتاد وپنج از صد مشتمین • بدر برج شرافتاد در ثمین • یکی قطره از بحر نیسان علم
بقدرت شده عین انسان علم • بسرتاج شاهی ودفتر سلیم • بحکمت طلبکار فیض حکیم
جلوسش بمقصد وتجدید کام • بادو لطف چون بار دهر مدام • مسخر نمود از عرب تا عجم •
باقلیم عثمان بقصر مود ضم • منظومه فی ترکی عجب مکر البس تعلیقی زاده وینه شهنامه کوم مکرم
اکر بوکوز واقعه قصه معلوم • یکیلوب مار سیدن اورجع دم • اغزنوکدرنوله هما اولورسه •
مروح حمالی ایله برقاج آدم • بونلردن قاعده اسلطان مراد خان وصفنده کی شمایل نامه نام کتابنده
بنز غیب قتلادمیشدر کم نظم دمیدرشاه ساززرم ایده لم عدد دفع عزم حزم ایده لم •
الوب ملک ایرانی بشدیدنا • ملوب نصب ایرلرده میرولیشا • نور الدین ایده لم بار عار •

بونلم

8

قوپالم جهان ایچره خوش یادکار • قونرلنک بیغدیسه صبا معلری • بیالم انک بیغدیغی یرلری
اکرالری اسلامدن اول اسیر • بزازاد اولدم صغیر و کبیر • ملک کم تبارکی آنکرا اوله •
نیورکبی هم بیندسر ورا اوله • بلان یاور بیسی کبی شهمار اولور • سوفا یوزلو بر زهردم دار اولور
القصه تبلیغی آده غل و غش قیدیدن آزاده لوح ذهنی آینه کبی زنک علایقدن •
ساده برفرزانه یکانه درکه اول برلری کبی خلط کلام امنیوب نظم و نثر بربرندن ایمازدر
انشای بدایع نشانننک شیوه سجع لطیف صحیح و مبنای اولدر غیری سیاق و سباقی مضبوط
سمت مرغوبله قصه پرداز • خصوصا کر علو درگاه والا کسیادن زیاده سموکه ستثنا
درد بوا وج بینی خوب نظم ایتمشدر • و هم نقصر ایدوب بو مجلده اکابر سلف طریقه
کتمشدر کویدیه کسی برتر آست اسمان • مکر بازشناسد از ریسمان • مکر ناشناس است یا جاهل است •
ویا خود چو من ابله و غافل است • که کوید چنین دیده ام در کتاب • که از ماه روشنتر است آفتاب
• شه ملک پادشاه جهان • فرمانکار کهان و مهان • سلطان محمد خان ابن
سلطان مرادخان ایلر اکری قلعه سی فتحنه طوغریلوب • بعد الفتح والتسخیر نظم ترکی نامه
تسطیر ایلدوکی ابیاتلا نظردن • بر قاچ بیتنک ایرادی مناسب کورلدی • یعنی که
بضاعه بی اضاعه سنی ابها ما • بو مجلده نقل و تسوید یه جرأت اولندی در مدح
مثلا آنان جو کفته نجم ترک خر طبع هیزم شکاف • شعر او آربالان حربی اکاف •
کنا بینی دیوا آده مانند نشست • بیغربرسری اوزره اولدیسرشت • معانی اوقویلوب سمنی
صورسک از رتبلی سرف اسمتی • اکر جنت طلب اولسه عذن اولور • موردسکی اکر دیندن کنو اولور
اوتاحو که بطللانی ظاهر ایکن • مسادی چوبو جهلا باهر ایکن • بولورنفسنی دایم اول بد اصل ها
چو مفعول منصوب اولور متصل • تنخقه عبائی یه اولور سوار • که اکه شرابه احر رو رکاره •
در خود درد شتی و ذکر شاهان ماضی بالالتفات [illegible] لطیط هنر و عطادی نم • که چون خریسمای حاتمی
بوبلی دولت اولدی چو دولت سناسوی [illegible] غم ابندی قدم دو غرا رنده [illegible] نشیندی جم کلا [illegible]
شجاعت سنا خلیفه نشان • زمین سای کم سمند شهان • الوب ال سلجوق نسل فنا
اولور نسل عباس عبوس عنا • فنی غزنویان محمود خوی • تنی طاهر نبان پاکیزه کوی •

لقب نامه دفتر کیقباد • ورق روزن اولدی بر باد باد • او فتنه اکر دیو بولاد وند
خداوند کوپال وکرز دکمه • اکر اولسه مذکور اکوان دیو • بلرزه یوان کیهان خدیو •
دماوند طاغندن یکه صاووره • حرز دشت الچنده خیمه صاووره • بیابانده سیاوخشی وحشی سنرز •
اکر رستمی کورسه رخشی سنرز نثر اکرچه که کتابنده کی ابیات بر بر سندن اعلی ایچو بونک کبی وارداث
در لکن اضاعهٔ اوقات خاطرسندهٔ بو مقدار ایله اکتفا محض دلنوازی و عرض الفقیر
علی الخصوص فارسی نظملری دخی واردر • اکثری مقبول و لطیف واپدارکر در • و هر بنده کی
تصرفات خاصه لری بشماردر • مع ذلک جمله سی پسند و تحسینه لایق و سزاوار دره
اما مولانا نطقی معیار امتحانه داخل و جز مهرهٔ کلامی انلرک جواهر دار النظامی الحلی عرصه
واصل اولموق لازم کلدوکده • بدیع قصه سی نطقی • نظم بدیع البیان منزله سنه تنزیل المستند
حقا کم رتبه انده بهر نوب سابق کبی • نظم و نثره متعلق اولان عیوبنی الحمستدر القصه کردم که احوال
عالم بهر جهتله و انذکرن • صاحب صدر اولان اکابر امم حب دنیا ایله مکدر و مفتون • حسنین
ستم ایسه اغنی وحسین دن فزون الرحیل ثم الرحیل صدالری ایسه آنا فانا مماح سمعه معروف
بما ناکه تشنح امطار سحابی یوزی صوینه خواب غفلتندن کوز اچدم • کندو کندومه پند ایدرک •
بو ابیات جواهر نثار معمولی خاکسار خلقتمه کهر ارصاچدم نظم ای که بنجاه رفت در خوابی • مکر
این پنج روز در یابی کی نماز توسنجاب شود نظم که بیکسر ذی درد و محرابی • فلاجرم سنینا
من معین الحکم ذخر ابتخت الطول کتاب کنه الاحبار تاکیفنه ال اوردم • مسلمین متعطشینه زلال
عرفان افاده سنی مناسب کوردم تا که مجلدات جباره که در دمجیسی تواریخ آل عثمان خداوندنی
احیار و صانع آثار کار دن استمناسنله تحریرینی انجامه ایرکوردم • امید وارم که حضرت •
کرد کار جل شانه عن الاظهار والاضمار اول مجلدات جهار مجال رغبت و اعتباره رکوکوندوکه اقالیم سبعه ده سیار
اوله خصوصا اشهار نسخه دلپذیر کوا اکر شیخ سعدینک کلستانی • و مولانا جامینک بهارستانی
کبی خزان و بهار • ولیالی و نهار • شهرهٔ خردمندان روزکار • و مایهٔ الافتخار دبیران منشی کردار •
ابد و کی محقق اوله • تا که والدین مرحومین غفران دثار • و حراین محمد وبین عرفان شعار حصوصاً نبکیک
مسعود ابیات فیضه کوششنر لنهار ایدن ستمی سول کرد کار فیض مخلص المحمد نام • اولان برادر فرمان برادر سعادت دار تیلم

۱۰۹

بهره دار اولوب مؤلف مجرم وکنهکار • ومصنف متأسف پریشان افکار • دنیا وآخرت
سعادتلرندن طول عمر که مقتضی الاوطار • وطلبنی علمیس دکر جمیل • ودعای جمیل • واجر جزیل
مزایاسندن بهره دار قلمه‌سی تحقق وتعیین بوله • حضرت خدای بزرکوار • عالم وواقف اسرار •
درکه بوناکیفدن مرادم تمتع منافع دینار • وترفع درهم ودینار دکلدر • زیرا که اکاه ویردارم
که جمیع کامروبار • ورغبت عرض وناموس ودمار • ودولت دنیا منقلب اولان طمطراق وآثار فانیه
عمر عاجل وظل زائلدر منتهیه اشبو تألیفدن بو در مقصود • اوله کوکلنده حزن وغم مفقود •
هر آدم خدا عنایت ایده • تعظیم الله رکوع وسجود • طول عمر وکمال علم وعمل
خلف صالح وصلاح وجود • صدقله توبه حسن خاتمه هم • شکر حمد ودو منزل محمود
بکا روزی قلوب ایده مولی • سیئاتم ورقلرین نابود • حکیم حوف جسرده منزلنی
اوله بن بنده‌دن خدا خشنود • کوریم نار دوزخ کشرین • کوزمه کریه اول اوددن دود
جنت لقاره مقام نمودم • دار دنیاده قل نکا شهود • تا زبان ایلیم تصوردن
چارسوی عملده کرم اوله سود • یا الهی بحق صحف امم • یا الهی بحق بهر موجود
بنی هم ملتک دعاسی ایله • بکا قیل لطف وجود نامعدود • واختلاف سکان روم ولجبان
منفیه عن ان مرزوم بتقدیر ملک حق وقیوم خفی اولمیه کم اصلنه قوم روم عیص بن
اسحق اولادندن ایدوکی معلوم • بر قوم پاک اعتقاد وصلابت رسوم درکه توحیدی
بسیار ومعتقدلری بیشمار • مؤمن وبی هنرکارلری • کرک شاب وکرک معاذ ثابت
صدق وایقان • وخلوص واذعان • اهلی عیب هدی للمتقین الذین یؤمنون بالغیب
نفس کریمه‌نه ناصد فلردر • نته که مبارزلری ومجاهدلرین کاه مثوبات غزا • وکاهی
دولت شهادت کبی رتبهٔ علیا • مراتبنه ملحقلردر • والحاصل سنه سبعین واربعمائه
مابینی اثنالرنده کی ملوک آل سلجوق که ملک رومه قدم باصدیلر قرق اللی بیلدن برو
اول سرحدلری تملک ایدن امرا ودانشمندیه ایلرکیدل وکهسنا اولوب کفار خاکساره
جهاد وغزادن خالی اولمدیلر • بعد الهجره الکی یوز بیلدن زیاده جه زمان مرورنده
عسکره اولا وعمر بن خطابدن جد اعلالری امیرزاده والک اوغلی امیر لقمان •

LITERATURE

Manuscripts

'Ālī, Muṣṭafā, *Künhü'l-aḫbār*, *Hs. or. quart. 1090* (Berlin, *Staatsbibliothek*) (*B*).
'Ālī, Muṣṭafā, *Künhü'l-aḫbār*, *Cod. 288 Warn.* (Leiden, University Library) (*L*).
'Ālī, Muṣṭafā, *Künhü'l-aḫbār*, *Ahmed III 3083* (Istanbul, Topkapı Sarayı).
An., *Cod. 1107 Warn.* (fragments of a translation in Turkish of the Bible).

Printed and edited sources

'Ālī, Muṣṭafā, *Ḫālatu'l-Ḳāhire* (Ed. A. Tietze, *Muṣṭafā 'Ālī's Description of Cairo of 1599*, Vienna 1975).
'Ālī, Muṣṭafā, *Künhü'l-aḫbār* 5 Vols. (Istanbul 1861-1868).
'Ālī, Muṣṭafā, *Mevā'idü'n-nefā'is fī ḳavā'idi'l-mecālis* (Ed. C. Baysun, Istanbul 1956).
'Ālī, Muṣṭafā, *Nuṣḥatu's-selāṭīn* (Ed. A. Tietze, *Muṣṭafā 'Ālī's Counsel for Sultans of 1581*, 2 Vols., Vienna 1979 and 1982).

Modern works

'Alī Cevād, *Memālik-i 'Os̱māniyyeniñ tāriḫ ve coġrafiyā luġatı*, 4 Vols. (Istanbul 1313).
Altundağ, Ş., 'Selim I', in: *İA* (*İslam Ansiklopedisi*) X, 423-434.
Atasoy, N., and F. Çağman, *Turkish Miniature Painting* (Istanbul 1974).
Atsız (*ed.*), *Âlî bibliyografyası* (Istanbul 1968).
Aumer, J., *Türkische Handschriften* (München 1875).
Babinger, F., *Die Geschichtsschreiber der Osmanen und ihre Werke* (*GOW*) (Leipzig 1927).
Blochet, E., *Catalogue des manuscrits Turcs*, 2 Vols. (Paris 1932).
Bosworth, C. E., *The Islamic Dynasties* (Edinburgh 1980, 2nd pr.).
Çağman, F., see Atasoy.
ad-Dağistānī, 'Alī Ḥilmī, *Fihristu'l-kutubi't-turkiyyati'l-mawǧūdati fi'l-kutubḫānati'l-ḫidiviyya* (Cairo 1306).
Encyclopedia of Islam (*EI*^{2}) (2nd edition, Leiden 1961 ff).
Eyüboğlu, E. K., *Onüçüncü yüzyıldan günümüze kadar Şiirde ve Halk Dilinde Atasözleri ve Deyimler*, II (Istanbul 1975).
Faroqhi, S., *Die Vorlage (telḫīṣ) des Gross-wesirs Sinan Paşa an Sultan Murad III* (Diss. Hamburg 1967).
Fekete, L., *Einführung in die osmanisch-türkische Diplomatik der türkischen Botmässigkeit in Ungarn* (Budapest 1926).
Fleischer, C. H., 'Gelibolulu Mustafa Âli Efendi, 1541-1600. A Study in Ottoman Historical Consciousness' (Diss. Princeton University 1982).
Fleischer, C. H., 'Royal Authority, Dynastic Cyclism, and "Ibn Khaldunism" in Sixteenth-Century Ottoman Letters', in: *Journal of Asian and African Studies*, XVIII (1983), 198-220.
Flemming, B., '*Der Cāmi' ül-meknūnāt*. Eine Quelle 'Ālīs aus der Zeit Sultan Süleymāns', in: H. R. Roemer and A. Noth (*ed.*) *Studien zur Geschichte und Kultur des Vorderen Orients* (Leiden 1981), 79-92.

Flemming, B., *Türkische Handschriften* I (Wiesbaden 1968).

Flemming, B., 'Turkse discussies omtrent het Christendom', in: *Historische betrekkingen tussen Moslims en Christenen, Midden Oosten en Islampublicatie* 9.

Flügel, G., *Die arabischen, persischen und türkischen Handschriften der k.-k. Hofbibliothek zu Wien* II (Vienna 1865).

Gibb, E. J. W., *A History of Ottoman Poetry*, 6 Vols. (London 1900-1909).

Goeje, M. J. de and P. de Jong, *Catalogus Codicum Orientalium Bibliothecae Academiae Lugduno Batavae (CCO)*, III (Leiden 1865).

Groot, A. H. de, 'The Legacy of a Seventeenth Century Orientalist' in: *Prilozi za orijentalnu filozofiju* of the Oriental Institute in Sarajevo, 30 (1980), 159-165.

Hammer, J. von, *Geschichte des Osmanischen Reiches*, 10 Vols. (Pest 1827-1835).

Haywood, E., *Watermarks, mainly of the 17th and 18th Centuries* in: *Monumenta Chartae Papyraceae* I (Hilversum 1950).

İslam Ansiklopedisi (*İA*) (Istanbul 1940ff).

Jahn, K., *Die Frankengeschichte des Rašīd ad-Dīn* (Vienna 1977).

Jong, P. de, see: de Goeje.

Juynboll, M. C., *Zeventiende eeuwsche beoefenaars van het Arabisch in Nederland* (Utrecht 1931).

Karatay, F. E., *Topkapı Sarayı Müzesi Kütüphanesi yazmalar kataloğu*, 2 Vols. (Istanbul 1961).

Kırzıoğlu, M. F., *Osmanlılar'ın Kafkas-elleri'ni fethi (1451-1590)* (Ankara 1976).

Ḳur'ānu karīm (*ed. Maǧma'u'l-buḥūṯi'l-Islāmiyyati bi'l-Azhari'š-šarīf*, Cairo 1967).

Levy, R., *The Tale of Marzuban* (London 1959).

Mendes da Costa (*ed.*), *Bibliotheek der Universiteit van Amsterdam. Catalogus der handschriften* II (Amsterdam 1902).

Ménage, V. L., 'The Beginnings of Ottoman Historiography', in: B. Lewis and P. M. Holt, *Historians of the Middle East* (London, New York and Toronto 1962), 168-179.

Ménage, V. L., 'Bidlīsī', in: *EI*², I, 1207-1208.

Ménage, V. L., 'Edirneli Ruhi'ye atfedilen Osmanlı tarihinden iki parça', in: *İsmail Hakki Uzunçarşılı'ya Armağan* (Ankara 1976), 311-333.

Ménage, V. L., 'Kemāl Pas̲h̲a-zāde', in *EI*², IV, 879-881.

Ménage, V. L., *Nes̲h̲rī's History of the Ottomans* (London 1964).

Mout, M. E. H. N., 'Calvinoturcisme in de zeventiende eeuw, Comenius, Leidse oriëntalisten en de Turkse Bijbel', in: *Tijdschrift voor Geschiedenis*, 16 (1978), 576-607.

Özge, M. S., *Eski harflerle basılmış Türkçe eserler kataloğu* II (Istanbul 1973).

Redhouse, *New Redhouse Turkish-English Dictionary* (2nd pr. Istanbul 1974).

Reshid, A., 'Ottoman-Mughul Relations during the seventeenth Century', in: *VI. Türk Tarih Kongresi (1961)*; *Kongreye sunulan bildiriler* (Ankara 1967), 533-545.

Rosenthal, F., *A History of Muslim Historiography* (3rd pr. Leiden 1968).

Rypka, J., *History of Iranian Literature* (transl. from the Czech and ed. by K. Jahn, Dordrecht 1968).

Schwartz, K., 'Die Sammlung türkischer Handschriften in der Staatsbibliothek Preussischer Kulturbesitz', in: *Acta Orientalia Hungarica*, 37 (1983), 111-120.

Sohrweide, H., 'Dichter und Gelehrte im osmanischen Reich (1453-1600). Ein Beitrag zur Kulturgeschichte', in: *Der Islam*, 46 (1970), 263-302.

Sohrweide, H., '*Enīs el-qulūb*: Ein verschollenes Werk des Historikers Muṣṭafā 'Ālī', in: *VIII. Türk Tarih Kongresi* (Ankara 1980), 983-991.

Steingass, F., *Persian-English Dictionary* (London 1892).

Tietze, A., 'Muṣṭafā 'Ālī of Gallipoli's Prose Style', in: *Archivum Ottomanicum*, 5 (1973), 297-319.

Tornberg, C. J., *Codices Arabici, Persici et Turcici Bibliothecae Regiae Universitatis Upsaliensis* (Upsala 1849).
Turan, Ş., 'Sinân Paşa', in *İA*, X, 666-675.
TTK, İstanbul kütüphaneleri tarih-coğrafya yazmalar kataloğları I, *Türkçe tarih yazmaları* (Istanbul 1943ff)
Uzunçarşılı, I. H., *Mekke-i Mükerreme emirleri* (Ankara 1972).
Vocabulaire Arabe-Français à l'usage des Étudiants (Beyrut 1883).
Wehr, H., *Arabic-English Dictionary* (ed. by J. M. Cowan and transl. from the German, 3rd ed., New York 1976).
Woodhead, C., *Ta'lîkî-zâde's Şehnâme-i hümâyûn. A History of the Ottoman Campaign into Hungary 1593-94*. (Berlin 1983).
Zambaur, E. de, *Manuel de généalogie et de chronologie pour l'histoire de l'Islam* (Hannover 1927).

INDEX

(Numbers refer to the pages of this study; numbers in italic type to the folios of the Leiden manuscript. Names are given as they occur in the English parts of the text; the translation of Turkish titles and technical terms is to be found on the page on which they occur or in the translation of the 'Preface'.)

1. Persons

2. Places, Countries, Nations, Dynasties, Literary Figures etc.

3. Works quoted or mentioned

4. Technical Terms and Topics